To Joe & Norma —
Consider this —
Be Spiritual,
Do Compassion.
And this —
Traditions and others
cannot define our
spirituality — we
define it ourselves!
                    Ed DeJean

A Leap to Everyday Spirituality

In the Eternal Atmosphere of Possibilities

Edgar K. DeJean

authorHOUSE®

AuthorHouse™
1663 Liberty Drive
Bloomington, IN 47403
www.authorhouse.com
Phone: 1-800-839-8640

First published by AuthorHouse 12/13/2011

ISBN: 978-1-4678-7057-3 (e)
ISBN: 978-1-4678-7058-0 (hc)
ISBN: 978-1-4678-7059-7 (sc)

Library of Congress Control Number: 2011961116

Printed in the United States of America

Contents

Foreword

By the Rev. Dr. William D. Peterson better known
as Pastor Bill, Friend Bill, or simply Bill

Since early in 1994 when I was called to be the pastor for Salem
(IN) Presbyterian Church, I have been blessed by learning from
– and with – Ed DeJean. Although sometimes the differing roles
and responsibilities of so-called "Clergy" and "Laity" can present
barriers to deep friendship or to "full disclosure" in matters of faith
(and doubt), with Ed I felt I was relating with a soul mate. Certainly
there were times when my role as Pastor/Session Moderator, and
his role as Parishioner/Clerk of Session influenced our interactions,
and indeed there were many times when we "agreed to disagree" on
matters theological and/or denominational, but not at the expense
of our friendship.

In 2000 spouse Kathy and I moved from Salem in *Washington*
County, Indiana, to Spokane in *Washington* State, but our connection
to Ed, his spouse Elinor, and their wonderful immediate and extended
family, continued thanks to Ed's faithful practice of writing what he
calls the Saturday Report. To be included in the e-list to receive these
whimsical updates on "All things DeJean" has become a continued
blessing in our lives. As with reading anything that comes "filtered
through" the creative mind of Dr. Edgar K. DeJean, the Saturday
Report elicits both guffaws and groans, but what a gift to family and
friends.

I write of my relationship with Ed so the reader who doesn't know
me, will recognize that this is not one of those "promo forewords"
from someone penning a few words as a courtesy to a colleague.
Rather I write as one whose own life and faith have been influenced
by this man.

In Ed DeJean I found a Mentor who was able to school this mid-life career changer (I was just coming out of seminary and Salem Presbyterian Church was the setting for both my Ordination as a Minister of the Word and Sacrament in the Presbyterian Church (USA), and my Installation as the Salem congregation's pastor). In Ed I found a seasoned Presbyterian with a lifetime of history in the denomination, and a "native son" of the region. What a gift to have the benefit of Ed's guidance.

More importantly even than Ed's guidance, was Ed's modeling of a committed life of loyalty to family, community, church, friends, et al. Here was a man who had retired following a distinguished career as an oral surgeon, and who could have rested on the laurels of his past accomplishments, but who still gave of himself to others in countless ways.

As this book (and indeed his series of books) reflects, Ed is not one who believes that everything we need to know about life and faith has already been revealed. Rather Ed puts into practice his conviction that we who are human and hence finite, are simply arrogant (and/or ignorant) if we claim to have all the answers about matters infinite in nature. In this respect you can be assured that I too get challenged when what I write, say, or share with Ed is a bit too "orthodox" for his tastes and convictions.

Ed has been – and continues to be – a blessing to me in my journey of life and faith. My hopes and prayers are that in reading this book you will experience such a blessing yourself. But be reminded, as he states in the last sentence of his Preface --

"This book ("A Leap to Everyday Spirituality, In the Eternal Atmosphere of Possibilities") is a candid invitation to explore our beliefs, not a request to agree with the author."

Preface

"You got to be very careful if you don't know
Where you're going, because you might not get there."
Yogi Berra

A preface (noun) is an introduction to a book, typically stating its subject, scope, or aims.

The material that follows herein is a series of blogs that I have morphed into a book. Please remember the word morph, it will appear frequently, perhaps ubiquitously.

In 2005 I produced a little book titled "A Belief System from the General Store." In that book I revealed how I had come by an orthodox Presbyterian belief system through the Beech Grove Presbyterian Church, augmented by loafing seminars with the men and boys of New Philadephia, Indiana at the H.H. McClellan General Store founded by him in 1866 and owned at this later, Loafing Seminar Period (1920's-40's) by his daughter (my grandmother) Edith McClellan Wiggs. In that book I traced my traditional belief system through a typical layperson's experience but noted that by the end of the 20th Century I was very aware that my belief system was morphing away from rigid orthodoxy.

In 2009 I produced another book titled "A Belief System from Beyond the Box." This book described my personal move beyond the box of traditionalism while noting the recent few years' 50% decline in the membership of the Presbyterian Church USA. In that book I countered the current claim that "Christianity must change or die" with a softer variant, "Christianity must morph to survive." One of my gentle suggestions in that book was that Christianity morph its conceptualization of the metaphysical force that renders purpose to all of existence from the Comprehensible God of the Bible Verse to the Incomprehensible Atmosphere of Possibilities of the Universe.

Over the past two years I have been in conversation with several peers regarding this morphing plus I have maintained a blog elaborating on and exploring ways to accomplish said morphing.

Here is the first paragraph of the first blog in the series:

It is Monday, March 18, 2009. As I checked my e-mail this morning I found an e-mail forwarded by my friend Bill Peterson, a Presbyterian pastor who is also a psychologist. Bill's friend, a professor at a university, had sent him a circulating, anonymous, e-mail list of 31 one liners titled, "For Those Who Take Life Too Seriously."

In keeping with Yogi Berra's advice I established a sense of direction for this series of blogs. First I would explore examples of taking life too seriously. Then expand to observations of taking one's beliefs too seriously followed by taking religion too seriously (religiosity) and finally arrive at taking theology inappropriately – where I suggest traditionalism has brought Christianity today.

This book ("A Leap to Everyday Spirituality, In the Eternal Atmosphere of Possibilities") is a candid invitation to explore our beliefs, not a request to agree with the author.

Address:

<edejean@blueriver.net>   <edgardejean@gmail.com>

Ponderings As Essays

1. It Is Monday

It is Monday, March 18, 2009. As I checked my e-mail this morning I found an e-mail forwarded by my friend Bill Peterson, a Presbyterian Pastor who is also a psychologist. Bill's friend, a professor at a university, had sent him a circulating, anonymous e-mail list of 31 one liners titled, "For Those Who Take Life Too Seriously."

One of them caught my eye because it is Monday –

"Monday is an awful way to spend 1/7 of your week."

Nonsensical? - of course. But some of the 31 were really clever. Like this one written in the days before digital photography -

"Everyone has a photographic memory. Some just don't have film."

I'll come back later to, "For those, who take life too seriously. "

Now, March 18 finds me twiddling my thumbs. I have just completed a three-year+ series of blogs that will soon be published as a book under the title. "A Belief System from Beyond the Box." This "Beyond the Box" series of blogs grew out of communications I shared following a 2005 book which described my belief system that evolved during my growing up in a country store: "A Belief System from the General Store."

Over the years I have pondered my belief system. I deny explicitly that I have obsessed my belief system. There is a great difference between pondering and obsessing. Through these decades of pondering I have concluded that my belief system is due an upgrade, as they say in the computer world. My recent communications with peers I know, and many peers I do not know, indicate that many hold this conclusion about their belief systems. The word *change* arises as we discuss our personal belief systems. I also hear the word *change* in discussions involving the institution through which we nurture our belief systems – "The church must change or it will die."

Change is difficult for most of us. Mark Twain recognized this: "Many are those we have known who were all for progress – it was change they couldn't tolerate."

Through this past several years, as I have heard this "change-or-die" expression so frequently, relative to the church, I have come to wonder if the problem could be more approachable if we softened the predictions to – "If we morph our belief systems, the church can morph and survive." "Morph and survive" sounds much more approachable than, "change or die."

What advice do we receive for responsive action on this "change or die" warning? Too often it is this vague admonition–

"You must think beyond the box."

What does the church currently tell us is in the box?

1. The Golden Rule, The Sermon on the Mount and unlimited, valuable, proven utterances.
2. The limitless ABCs of the Comprehensible God of the Bible Verse **as selected and <u>accepted</u>** by previous and present cultures.

What do I determine to be in the box?

1. The Golden Rule, The Sermon on the Mount and unlimited, valuable, proven utterances.
2. The inhibiting ABCs of the Comprehensible God of the Bible Verse **as selected and <u>imposed</u>** by previous and present cultures.

My working formulary for these ABCs follows:

A. Factious Fundamentals and Doctrines
B. Embellished Stories and Myths.
C. Outmoded Knowledge and Cultures.

My concern is that the box contains inhibiting ABCs by which cultures have tried over the centuries to render God comprehensible to humans – who can conceptualize, although not comprehend -- God.

What is beyond the box? - the Incomprehensible God of the Universe, "the atmosphere of possibilities that lures the Earthen histories upslope." (Rolston)

In his book, "Genes, Genesis and God, Their Origins in Natural and Human History," Holmes Rolston III lures us beyond the box with this quote (p.367).

"The divine spirit is the giver of life, pervasively present over the millennia. God is the atmosphere of possibilities, the metaphysical environment, in, with, and under first the natural and later also the cultural environment, luring the Earthen histories upslope."

Here follows my layman's interpretation of Dr. Rolston's thesis that he so thoroughly explains in a scholar's language.

Expanding knowledge of genes, DNA, and evolution of life forms, has resulted in macro understandings of the **how** of biogenesis. But there is that stage in the biogenetic process where the human mind remains at a micro understanding of the **why** within the informational component of the process. Obviously the Planet Earth's "sea of soup" for the formation of life was perfect for the how. So where did *the information* reside that triggered the chain reaction - the **why did it start**? Is there a metaphysical something, a stimulator, within, or behind, the informational component that instills and then maintains value and purpose in the all of life?

My study of his book tells me that Dr.Rolston writes of this stimulator. It is the atmosphere of possibilities. It is God. This stimulator is not a directive, theistic force. It does not push or pull life upslope. Dr. Rolston states that it is, "luring the earthen histories upslope."

At the time I discovered Dr. Rolston's concept - God is the Atmosphere of Possibilities - I was describing in my blogs the morphing of my belief system from the Comprehensible God of the Bible Verse to the Incomprehensible God of the Universe. Serendipity handed me this gap-filling element for my conceptualization of God. I have long realized that the human cannot comprehend God but it is essential to have conceptualizations beyond "God is Great, God is Good." Thus I became response-able to: **The Incomprehensible God of the Universe, the Atmosphere of Possibilities.**

The question occurred – what is it that ties us to the Comprehensible God of the Bible Verse? It is the "what has been." More broadly stated it is the **Climate of Cultures**.

Thus to think beyond the box, we must expand our belief systems beyond the Climate of Cultures (the what has been) into the Atmosphere of Possibilities (the what can be!).

There are not two Gods, of course. It is my conceptualization that is changing from - the Comprehensible God of the Bible Verse, the Climate of Cultures to - the Incomprehensible God of the Universe, the Atmosphere of Possibilities.

As I review this Monday morning blog in preparation for a return to the phrase, "For those who take life too seriously," I realize that we cannot discern life qualitatively (the meaning of "too seriously") until we have defined life objectively, within the following question -

Is life accidentally incidental or is life intentionally purposeful?

2. Life – Accidental or Intentional?

Accidental? What about DNA? Could something so complex be accidental?

Intentional? What about virulent organisms? Dinosaurs? Could deadly organisms or such bizarre creatures be intentional?

Please note that the word created does not appear in this heading as an opposite to the word accidental. Of course life was created when molecules of specific substances combined into an organism that, through the miracle of DNA, could replicate into an identical, live organism. When the word "created" opposes the word "accidental" (or "happened") the human mind transposes the word created into the word creator, capitalizes the c and likens the word Creator to the word God. This is an oversimplification.

In "Genes, Genesis and God," Dr. Rolston takes the reader all the way back to DNA in the formation of life and then one step further. He asks what is the information-transfer mechanism through which the life process transmits not only **form** but value (**function**) and purposefulness (**metaphysical function**)? How does one explain the transference of value and purposefulness within the biogenetic process unless there is some incomprehensible-metaphysical, information transmission?

It is discouraging in an enlightened era to find continuing opposition to the knowledge that life forms do, and will continue to, evolve as changing physical forms. However, there is a hopeful sign. The opposition is itself evolving. Those who once denied the process are now conceding that the evolutionary process exists but insist that it is not a random process of natural selection but a process controlled and directed by "Intelligent Design." This is anthropomorphic jargon. This is an attempt to reduce the Incomprehensible Atmosphere of Possibilities to a thinking, human-like designer. No, applying the limiting conceptualizations intelligent and intentional to the Atmosphere of Possibilities renders God too small.

Because I cannot comprehend how replicating DNA came to be does not negate the fact of its existence. Because I cannot comprehend how metaphysical information produces the transfer of value and purpose throughout all of life does not deny the process. Although I can merely conceptualize God to be the Stimulator, the Atmosphere of Possibilities; I do indeed comprehend the value, purpose and seriousness of life - every minute of it.

Before we go back to the phrase, "For those who take life too seriously," I shall share a very short story in the next blog.

3. A Story I Heard.

My wife Elinor and I live in a comfortable retirement community composed of super people loaded with superlative stories. At dinner recently a fellow resident was telling our table that her ancestors had emigrated from Norway and Sweden to Minnesota by way of ships that landed in Louisiana.

When one set of her great grandparents met and married they

settled in a small Minnesota town where, as typical townsfolk, they established with the town and with the church.

In this town in a later year a man labeled "the town drunk" did not make it to his quarters on a frigid night and was found frozen to death the next day.

The church board refused to permit his burial in its cemetery, the only one in town. "After all, this was a man who had chosen to be the town drunk."

After much effort - against continuing, rigid refusal - our fellow resident's great grandfather solved the problem for the town by burying the man on land he owned.

Some years later the church found it needed to expand its cemetery. The great grandfather graciously gave the church a generous strip of his land that happened to border the existing cemetery and happened to contain the remains of the man who had frozen to death.

The church board had forgotten – but -- surprise, surprise – "the man who had chosen to be the town drunk" was now buried in their cemetery.

The question: "Is it possible to take beliefs too seriously?"

4. Do Unto Others -

We make two judgment calls when we opine that someone is taking their beliefs about life too seriously. The first call is qualitative - their action is beyond normal. The second call is quantitative - their action is **too** far beyond normal.

Both of these judgments are valid, of course, because our own beliefs about life are normal in quality and amount. Thus we can determine when those who take their beliefs too seriously are taking their beliefs too seriously. Not only can we determine the when, we can calibrate how much too serious "their too seriously" is.

With these faux guidelines stated, I'll remove tongue from cheek and come back to reality.

As I proposed earlier that the phrase, "those who take life too seriously." is actually about beliefs and not life, I would propose further that the phrase "too seriously" does not concern beliefs about life but more narrowly aims at religious beliefs.

When does a belief become a religious belief?

When we state, "The physical Universe is an unlimited space containing mass-energy in increments from atoms to galaxies," we are describing our beliefs about physical form.

When we state, "Replicating life within the Universe might have been created by a series of physical forces, e.g. lightning strikes into a 'sea of soup,' we are describing our varying beliefs about physical function."

When we state, "Replicating life within the universe has evolved to the status of recognizing that the universe has value and life has purpose," we are describing our diverse beliefs about metaphysical function.

Homo sapiens, through language, has taken this process to the point of verbal definition and *beliefs about metaphysical function* are labeled **religious beliefs**.

The human can express beliefs because it has intellect. A dictionary lists intellect as:

a. The ability to learn and reason; the capacity for knowledge and understanding.

b. The ability to think abstractly or profoundly.

My mentioning intellect here is to introduce its connection to metaphysical function. Intellect relates to the metaphysical but no human's intellect comprehends the metaphysical – no layperson's, no historian's, no scholar's, no theologian's, no scientist's. The most abstract or profound thought can merely conjecture or conceptualize - not understand, comprehend or "know" the metaphysical or its functionary – however/whatever that may be.

Intellect came to the human species over hundreds of thousands of years. Intelligent actions gradually, oh so slowly, replaced instinctual reactions. The first (seminal) evidence of human intelligence had to be the recognition that others of the human species also had intelligence.

This approach brings me to the conceptualization that compassion (being responsible to/with fellow humans) was the first purpose for life discovered by the human and religious beliefs (being response-able to some metaphysical functionary) came eons later.

Over these eons myriad theological mind-sets evolved to describe the nature of the response-able relationship between the human and the metaphysical functionary. Abbreviated descriptions of the Judeo and Christian mind-sets follow:

Judeo - this theological mindset conjectured that during a vague span in human development about four millennia ago the one and only metaphysical functionary injected a **1 milligram** dose of theistic stimulant into the members of a specific tribe of humans and as a response they *comprehended* (their term) the functionary to be Yahweh. They developed many oral accounts and scrolls that authenticated their *comprehension*.

Christian - some two millennia ago another theological mindset deduced that the original 1 milligram dose was a failure and it determined that the metaphysical functionary on this subsequent occasion injected members of multiple tribes with a **3 milligram** dose of theistic stimulant - one milligram each for the Father, the Son and the Holy Ghost. This became their religious belief - their *comprehension* of the metaphysical functionary. They added to the original scrolls and developed an "inerrant" book that authenticates their *comprehension* to this day.

What I shall offer is not comprehension. It is conjecture – pure conceptualization if you will.

I believe that compassion (being responsible to/with fellow humans) was the first purpose for life discovered by the human and religious beliefs (being response-able to some metaphysical functionary) came eons later.

Why, then, has the human forsaken the value and purposefulness of compassion that permitted humanity to evolve and survive, and has become obsessed with taking religious beliefs too seriously (e.g. religious chaos, religious wars)?

5. As We Would That Others –

Over the ages the great religions, as well as many secular groups within humanity, have condensed their belief systems to succinct standards for life.

One such standard has attained near-universal status:

"Do unto others as we would that others do unto us."

A more elaborate form of the statement is:

"Treat others only in ways that you're willing to be treated in the same exact situation."

This standard in its many forms has come to be known as "The Golden Rule."

The writer, Edwin Markham, has given the rule vitality and purpose in the following quotation:

"We have committed the Golden Rule to memory;
Let us now commit it to life."

The term Golden Rule is so universally accepted that it is probably to no avail to note that this name conveys absolutely *no descriptive* value. In spite of that I would be brave (naïve) enough to offer the suggestion that consideration be given to a change of name to:

"The Universal Rule for Human Compassion."

Perhaps this roils the waters of tradition enough for one blog?

6. Do Unto Us.

With the final phrase of the Universal Rule for Human Compassion - Do Unto Us, we have completed the measuring stick, the template, by which we can gauge the quality and quantity of the religious nature of ourselves and others, including those whom we judge, correctly or incorrectly, as taking their religious concepts too seriously.

Did God, as the Atmosphere of Possibilities, initiate the life process? Does God, as Encompassing Love, maintain the life process? Will God, as Universal Compassion, lure the Earthen histories upslope?

These conceptualizations are not intended to be a contemporary trinity. They simply happen to be three descriptions of the metaphysical information essential to the genesis and maintenance of the awesome life process containing not only value, but purpose. As one attempts to conceptualize the Atmosphere of Possibilities it seems natural to conceive (form a mental image of) God as a Source of information rather than a Force of direction. However, Yahweh was directive in the extreme. The Comprehensible God of the Bible Verse, the Climate of Cultures, is deemed personally directive by many. Logic added to intellect would suggest that the Incomprehensible God of the Universe, the Atmosphere of Possibilities, lures via compassion rather than directing via coercion.

I would propose here that humanity's belief systems can be structured in such a way that we recognize valid qualitative and quantitative attributes of religious practices.

As I have struggled with my belief system I have thought of it as involving the relationships of three entities; an Incomprehensible Metaphysical Functionary*, a comprehensible humanity and a bewildering self within the fragile Nature of the Universe.

What kind of a Metaphysical Functionary, what kind of a humanity, what kind of a self?

Here again is my belief statement:

"I believe that the Incomprehensible God of the Universe is an Atmosphere of Possibilities within which the human can be a response-able steward to and for the Incomprehensible God – and responsible to and with comprehensible humanity, including self, in God's **Kindom.**"

It is my hope that this belief statement encompasses The Rule for Universal Compassion:

"Do unto others as we would that others do unto us."

* Those who claim to be atheists would not include *nonexistent* God into such a relationship by any name. Neither do I claim that the Metaphysical Functionary (the Atmosphere of Possibilities, God) will break physical laws, e.g. "sun standing still," human parthenogenesis (one human precursor only), hypostatic union (divine plus human), the resurrection of dead bodies. I would deem the Atmosphere of Possibilities to be the Metaphysical Information that gives the Universe being plus giving life value and purposefulness beyond human ability to comprehend the process.

7. Back to the "Too Seriously" Dilemma.

This dilemma has two parts.
First – The problem –
Too often, too many of us take "our" religion too seriously.

Second – The solution –

Too many of us fail to recognize the solution - The Rule of Universal Compassion, The Golden Rule.

The previous blog "3. A Story I Heard," (about burial of the man who froze to death) is an example of the problem portion of the dilemma.

Next I present another experience that I suggest indicates what could be part of the way to a solution.

On Friday, March 13, 2009 I was watching Bill Moyer's Journal on PBS. His guest was Karen Armstrong who described a current project in which she is a principal.

First I ask you to go to this web address:

http://charterforcompassion.com/about

Here you can read the Charter for Compassion excerpt plus much more.

Following your investigation of this material, some of which I post here, I will list the address for a transcript of Bill Moyer's conversation with Karen Armstrong on the Bill Moyer Journal, March 13, 2009.

About
The Charter for Compassion

The Charter for Compassion is a collaborative effort to build a peaceful and harmonious global community. Bringing together the voices of people from all religions, the Charter seeks to remind the world that while all faiths are not the same, they all share the core principle of compassion and the Golden Rule. The Charter will change the tenor of the conversation around religion. It will be a clarion call to the world.

Over the next months this site will be open for the world to contribute to Charter for Compassion. Using innovative group decision-making software, people of all faiths, from all across the globe, will contribute their words and stories on a website designed specifically for the Charter. A Council of Conscience, made up of religious thinkers and leaders, will craft the world‚Äôs words into the final version of the Charter. The document will not only speak to the core ideas of compassion but will also address the actions all segments of society can take to bring these ideas into the world more fully. The Charter for Compassion will then be signed by religious leaders of all faiths at a large launch event, followed by a series of other events to publicize and promote the Charter around the world.

The Charter for Compassion will not be a new organization. There are hundreds of existing organizations around the world already working tirelessly in the name of compassion and interfaith dialogue. Our goal is to highlight these groups in effort to raise the profile of their work.

The Charter will show that the voice of negativity and violence so often associated with religion is the minority and that the voice of compassion is the majority. Through the participation of the grassroots, people around the world will expect more out of religious leaders and one another. In doing so, the Charter will shift conceptions of religion for all people.

––

The web address of the March 13, 2009 Moyer-Armstrong conversation can be copied and pasted to the reader's web browser:

http://www.pbs.org/moyers/journal/03132009/transcript3.html
The quote and transcript noted above describe a means to confront those who haughtily proclaim their religious concepts so inerrant as to render the concepts of all others deficient in value or even as having no value.

Stated in another manner:

"The easy confidence with which I know another man's religion is folly should teach me to suspect that my own could be also."
Mark Twain, A Biography

When I proclaim that mine are the only religious concepts with value I am taking my religion too seriously. The church board members devalued their individual persons and intellects when they ignored the compass of compassion and refused a burial site for the man who had frozen to death. Whether it is one fellow human with a different life style from ours, or millions of humans holding religious concepts that differ from ours, we all diminish God's Kindom when we fail to apply the Rule of Universal Compassion.

As individuals, as communities, as societies, as cultures, as religions – ad infinitum – believers can take their religious concepts so seriously that they pervert compassion into religious competition, even fanaticism, even unto death - their own (e.g. suicidal terrorists) and/or the deaths of their victims.

In these blogs through examples from my past, and similar experiences of others, I plan to explore the current world in which too many take their religious beliefs too seriously. How can these perversions be reversed for those trapped within such excesses?

Just as I have posited that the only way to morph the church to survival is for its members to morph their belief systems, I find it essential that taking religion too seriously, from trivial degrees to the tragic, must be examined so that morphing away from such excesses can be accomplished.

If I am willing to injure another human; physically - psychologically, emotionally, overtly or covertly; I am lacking in compassion. Compassion is the template that renders the human, human. All major world religions add to the template the sane principle of compassion - doing to others as we wish done to us. If I commit harm within the secular realm, I am lacking in human integrity. If I do such an act out of religious reasons, I am lacking in religious sanity. Rational humans do irrational acts when the driving force is misinterpretation of that accepted as secular normalcy or valid religious belief.

There are innumerable levels of being too religious. I do not claim authority concerning these various levels. It is easy to recognize the extreme. It is more difficult to recognize the subtle.

There is an extreme difference between the religious and the too religious. The Rule of Universal Compassion is safe in the hands of the religious and most of the secular. Any rules are at risk in the hands of the too religious – even the Ten Commandments.

8. Even - The Ten Commandments.

The Rule of Universal Compassion is truly universal. It fits all of humanity - religious or secular, believers of this or believers of that.

Its Decalogue counterpart, known as the Ten Commandments, is distinctly a part of the Judeo-Christian religion.

When it comes to abusing the Ten Commandments within separation of church and state, there are two groups. First are the Religious who know the commandments well, can recite them with fluent fervor, and apply them with compassion. Second are the Too Religious who can't recite more than three of the commandments but demand the posting of all ten everywhere.

Some years ago posting the Ten Commandments in public places reached fever pitch. In 2003 Chief Justice Roy Moore of the Alabama Supreme Court was suspended by the states ethics panel for refusing to obey a federal court order directing him to remove the two-ton stone tablet of the Commandments he had snuck into the rotunda of a state judicial building in Alabama.

Closer to home during that period, the County Commissioners of my home county were smitten with an obsession to post said Commandments in the County Courthouse. They were less ostentatious than Justice Moore. They settled on a two-pound frame with a paper copy rather than a two-ton monument. Their legal counsel advised them that the project was probably acceptable, but suggested that they seek advice from the State Legislature Representative from their district. They did so.

The State Legislator offered a minor caveat, "It's OK, but don't post them in too prominent a place." Did he have in mind the furnace room? The commissioners chose a dimly lit corner of the Courthouse lobby. Do I have to explain to the reader how minimally removed this spot was from "too prominent?" Do I need to elaborate on the prolonged legal proceedings, legal costs, and court costs that ended with the framed document removed from the Courthouse (the dimly lit corner) and the County Commissioners paying $15,000.00 in legal and court costs for the lesson learned.

A sage farmer who lived 12 miles from the courthouse observed, "I don't need to go to the courthouse to read the Ten Commandments, but my trip to the county seat would be a lot smoother if those fool commissioners had spent that $15,000.00 on filling the 3,000 pot holes between my house and the courthouse."

Sometimes those we elect to fill potholes take their religion too seriously.

9. Why the Fervor?

When there are over 600 rules (simple and complex, sound and quirky) in the Old Testament, I often wonder why we moderns put so much effort into posting a certain ten of them. I also wonder why we put so much emotion into posting rules of a specific religious faith in public places open to peoples of all faiths or non-faiths. Just to refresh my memory here are the ten straight from Deuteronomy (King James Version – from which the Shorter Catechism cometh):

1. Thou shalt have none other gods before me.
2. Thou shalt not make thee any graven image.
3. Thou shalt not take the name of thy Lord thy God in vain.
4. Keep the Sabbath day to sanctify it.
5. Honor thy father and thy mother.
6. Thou shalt not kill.
7. Neither shalt thou commit adultery.
8. Neither shalt thou steal.
9. Neither shalt thou bear false witness against thy neighbor.
10. Neither shalt thou covet.

When the Ten Commandments were transferred from the King James version of the Old Testament to the Shorter Catechism they appear as Question 43. When I did a small 2005 book titled "A Belief System from the General Store." I reworded the Questions of the Shorter Catechism from 17th Century culture and language to 21st Century norms. Here they are as reworded:

Q. 43. What are the Ten Commandments that have come to us from the writers of the Old Testament?

1. There is only one God of all that is.
2. God is a Spirit that cannot be imaged or manipulated.
3. Do not call God's name in vain. Call God's name in love.
4. Every day is holy. Pay special attention to the Sabbath.
5. Honor the person hood of everybody. Honor the parenthood of your father and mother.
6. Do not kill or harm the bodies nor diminish the spirits of your fellows.
7. Do not cheat anyone, especially those with whom you are in relationship.
8. Do not steal anything, visible or invisible, which belongs to another.

9. Do not say anything that will harm another inappropriately.
10. Do not covet anything, whether it is yours or someone else's.

Recently I received correspondence from a friend sending me a letter from his friend who had attended an Elderhostel near Kotzebue, Alaska - thirty miles north of the Artic Circle. Kotzebue is part of the tribal territory of the Inupiats.

During the course of the Elderhostel, the friend learned – and shared – his impression that the ten Inupiat values have much in common with the values stated in the biblical literature. The Inupiat ten follow:

1) Show respect to others - each person has a special gift
2) See connections – all things are related
3) Honor your elders – they show you the way in life
4) Accept what life brings – you cannot control many things
5) Have patience – some things cannot be rushed
6) Pray for guidance – many things are not known
7) Live carefully – what you do will come back to you
8) Take care of others – you cannot live without them
9) Share what you have – giving makes you richer
10) Know who you are – you are a reflection of your family

Please notice, however, that the Inupiat values are compassion in a universal sense and not religious values in a restrictive sense. There is all the difference in the world.

10. Religion in New Philadelphia.

Being "born and raised" require no effort from the individual, up to a point. An individual's family and community supply the necessary energy for the first several months.

I was born and raised a Southern Indiana Rural Hoosier. This had some disadvantages but I have always found them outweighed by benefits. I was born in the village of New Philadelphia in Franklin

Township eight miles East of Salem, the county seat of Washington County.

New Philadelphia was not a crossroad, it was a half a crossroad. It was a "T" where Main Street started at East-West Lexington Road and ran North. The McClellan General Store and residence, built just after the Civil War, occupied the Northeast angle of the "T." My grandmother Edith McClellan Wiggs, daughter of Harry H. McClellan, founder of the store, was its proprietor during my "growing up" years. A residence and a Methodist Church filled the Northwest angle of the "T."

Main Street extended North from the "T" for three houses on each side and then into farmland. Eight houses West of the "T" and six to the East, including the one room schoolhouse plus six barns completed the structural census of the village.

In the glory days, long before my birth, there had been a Presbyterian Church, a doctor's office, three general stores, a tannery and currier, a wagon manufacturer, a lodge hall, and more houses. The school had been a two-story, combination grade and high school until a tornado reduced it to a one-room school for the eight elementary grades.

It should be noted that even in the glory days there was no post office. That service was always rendered in the general store, or in a private residence, as a substation of the Salem Post Office. My grandfather Edgar Wiggs, deceased before I was born, had been postal carrier on a route from New Philadelphia further to the East.

Before I was born the Presbyterian Church had been razed and rebuilt, four miles East in a very rural grove of beech trees. We were ecumenical. My two older sisters and I attended the Methodist Sunday School in New Philadelphia and hurried home, two houses East, to accompany the family, in a blue Nash Four Door Sedan with two jump seats, to worship at the Beech Grove Presbyterian Church.

Ethnicity and race were not a presence nor big items for discussion in our community. There was one nice lady of dark complexion but whispers that she was "part Indian" were best "squashed like a potato bug," to use my grandmother's approach to solving contentious matters.

Within the religious climate of the community there was little talk about people "taking their religion too seriously." Folks generally held to one of three categories of religion. The first was "regular religion." The second was "holy roller religion." The third was "no religion."

Some folks used the term, "gone crazy over religion," but that phrase was not acceptable in my grandmother's household.

As I recall the predominate community opinion concerning those who took their religion too seriously would have been, "they're more a curiosity than a problem."

However, I offer this - those were different times and that was a different place.

11. The Chicken or the Egg?

The human has delighted for untold centuries in the conundrum, "Which came first the chicken or the egg?"

The scientific facts presented by undeniable evolutionary study years ago rendered this puzzle moot.

An inordinately larger puzzle has gone unnoted. No matter what creation story humans ascribe to they assume that the human was "created religious," i.e. responsive to the metaphysical. Since all of existence has value and purpose through the metaphysical a relationship has indeed existed through the long travail from unaware animal to aware human. But within that travail I would suggest that compassion appeared within human awareness ahead of religion. I make this blog extremely short for emphasis and repeat the ending paragraph from Blog 4 -

"Why, then, has the human forsaken the value and purposefulness of compassion that permitted humanity to evolve and survive, and has become obsessed with taking religious beliefs too seriously (e.g. religious chaos, religious wars)?"

12. Humanism or Theism?

Here is a quote from Blog 4, "I believe that compassion (being responsible to/with fellow humans) was the first purpose for life discovered by the human and religious beliefs (being response-able to some metaphysical functionary) came eons later."

A question derives naturally from the quote above: Which came first, humanism or theism? Humanism is a study of the being and nature of the human. Theism is a study of the being and nature of theos, the metaphysical functionary, the incomprehensible God of the universe, the atmosphere of possibilities. It is only one small step to ontology, the branch of metaphysics dealing with the nature of being.

Thereafter, ontological tradition holds that our next step is a detour to visit "Saint Anselm of Canterbury (1033-1109) the outstanding Christian philosopher and theologian of the eleventh century. He is best known for the celebrated "ontological argument" for the existence of God in chapter two of the *Proslogion*, but his contributions to philosophical theology (and indeed to philosophy more generally) go well beyond the ontological argument." *Stanford Encyclopedia of Philosophy*.

Note: With proper reverence for Saint Anselm's efforts and respect for his dedication, I still encourage the pragmatism of a prerequisite awareness of Hans Christian Anderson's tale, "The Emperor's New Clothes," to those who undertake an understanding of Anselm's "Ontological Argument."

Here follows a quote from the *Stanford Encyclopedia of Philosophy* which I hope is an adequate presentation of Anselm's thesis:

"Looking back on the sixty-five chapters of complicated argument in the Monologion, Anselm found himself wishing for a simpler way to establish all the conclusions he wanted to prove. As he tells us in the preface to the Proslogion, he wanted to find a single argument that needed nothing but itself alone for proof, that would by itself be enough to show that God really exists; that he is the supreme good, who depends on nothing else, but on whom all things depend for their being and for their well-being; and whatever we believe about the divine nature. (P, preface)

That "single argument" is the one that appears in chapter 2 of the Proslogion. (We owe the curiously unhelpful name "ontological argument" to Kant. The medievals simply called it "that argument of Anselm's" [argumentum Anselmi].)

The proper way to state Anselm's argument is a matter of dispute, and any detailed statement of the argument will beg interpretative questions. But on a fairly neutral or consensus reading of the argument (which I shall go on to reject), Anselm's argument goes like this. God is "that than which nothing greater can be thought"; in other words, he is a being so great, so full of metaphysical oomph, that one cannot so much as conceive of a being who would be greater than God. The Psalmist, however, tells us that "The fool has said in his heart, 'There is no God'" (Psalm 14:1; 53:1). Is it possible to convince the fool that he is wrong? It is. All we need is the characterization of God as "that than which nothing greater can be thought." The fool does at least understand that definition. But whatever is understood exists in the understanding, just as the plan of a painting he has yet to execute already exists in the understanding of the painter. So that than which nothing greater can be thought exists in the understanding. But if it exists in the understanding, it must also exist in reality. For it is greater to exist in reality than to exist merely in the understanding. Therefore, if that than which nothing greater can be thought existed only in the understanding, it would be possible to think of something greater than it (namely, that same being existing in reality as well). It follows, then, that if that than which nothing greater can be thought existed only in the understanding, it would not be that than which nothing greater can be thought; and that, obviously, is a contradiction. So that than which nothing greater can be thought must exist in reality, not merely in the understanding."

Here follow this layman's deductions from the previous long quote:

The human recognizes space and outer space. Is "outer space" reality or an oxymoron?

The human recognizes the physical and the metaphysical. Is "the metaphysical" reality or an oxymoron?

The physical has being. Does the metaphysical have being?

Is the metaphysical functional? Is there a metaphysical functionary?

Anselm says the metaphysical functionary is God, a he with being which Anselm characterizes as "that than which nothing greater can be thought. "Seems to me, "that than which nothing greater can be thought," would be incomprehensible. How then do we comprehend that God is a he and is a being, and is greater than something else?

Tillich appears to be on much firmer ground (no pun) when he describes God as the "Ground of All Being."

I'll just tag along with the thought that the Metaphysical Functionary is the Incomprehensible God of the Universe luring earthen histories upslope – dressed appropriately for the occasion in the fabric of possibilities rather than unintelligible threads of hyperbole i.e. the Emperor's new clothes.

13. Caught in the Act.

I'll admit it. I asked the question, Humanism or Theism? and promptly went off on the ontological tangent of questioning Anselm of Canterbury (1033-1109), who spent a lifetime of study searching for a concise, one sentence proof of God. Worse still, using a fairy tale by Hans Christian Anderson as my sole reference, I blithely subsumed Anselm's toils into my own searching sentence comparing this fabric of possibilities to unintelligible threads of hyperbole.

I apologize to the reader currently and to Saint Anselm retroactively. I do not claim to have spent a lifetime of scholastic search for a concise proof of God. I would more liken my lifetime to one of waiting for natural selection to present me with a belief system that maintains me responsible to humanity and self and later sustains me response-able to God. Thus as I approached the contrast of humanism and theism I permitted the natures of their beings (ontology) to divert me to theology and to Saint Anselm. So often when I turn to study theology I find that those who write about it use theistic verbiage unintelligible to those of us who function in the humanistic world. They clothe "the that than which nothing greater can be thought" God in their tedious threads of hyperbole. I envision the Incomprehensible God of the Universe clothed in the simple fabric of possibilities.

It is my deduction that this is the reason why humanists, watching the "too" religious processions of theists, can observe with the little boy, "The emperor has no clothes."

Again this quote from Blog 4 used as the first paragraph of Blog 12: "I believe that compassion (being responsible to/with fellow humans) was the first value and purpose for life discovered by the human and religious beliefs (being response-able to some metaphysical functionary) came eons later."

This belief does not come to me from the Judeo-Christian Scriptures. To the contrary the scriptural account tells me that the human was created perfect by God, although not perfectly enough to resist falling from perfection. God also planted a tree of the knowledge of good and evil. However the good knowledge was not strong enough to overcome the evil knowledge so eating of the tree's fruit meant, "you shall die." The third shortcoming in the account was a serpent, source unknown, which had no respect for perfect creatures or good knowledge, but enough power of persuasion to overcome both.

The process of species natural selection has given Homo sapiens physical form over millions of years. The process of intellectual cognitive development has given Homo sapiens compassionate performance over hundreds of thousands of years. The process of individual spiritual discernment has given me a system of belief in the Incomprehensible God of the Universe, the Atmosphere of Possibilities, over my lifetime. Within these three processes I can conceptualize that there are possibilities of informational transfers, which I cannot comprehend, between the metaphysical and life - which transfers give value and purpose to all of life.

I can neither believe, conceptualize nor comprehend that the metaphysical can or does break the natural laws of the Universe by causing: the sun to "stand still," human birth through parthenogenesis, incarnation, reincarnation, dead bodies to resurrect or live bodies to ascend.

All these ages humans have been searching to "link" the human to lower forms of life. We have "discovered "that "link" multiple times. There is no specific "link" because the evolutionary process has been a continuum over millions of years.

But actually there are two missing links. We have been looking in the wrong eons for them. The first is not millions of years old. It is billions of years old. At some nanosecond 3.4 billion years ago (give or take a few million) as a culmination of the interplay of huge meteorites striking planet Earth, freezing, thawing, primordial seas of soup, lightning etc. etc. some RNA replicated into identical RNA and life came to the earth. Later DNA and proteins formed one cell life and the human was on its way. The human can conceptualize that information from somewhere gave RNA its nudge to replicate. The RNA was physical. The information (the nudge) was metaphysical. Thus we discovered (better stated - conceptualized) the first link as that metaphysical information which nudged matter and energy into life with its resultant value.

The human can only imagine that the second link functioned but we will never discover how or when it performed its linking. The second link achieved "linkdom" over millions of years while that metaphysical information (nudge) infused purpose into life. In the next blog we'll try to determine at what point that purpose inculcated compassion.

14. Discovered: The Compassion Link

Way back in Blog #4. "Do Unto Others, " I spoke of life as attaining special value and purpose when life achieved intellect. Here is that statement in quotes:

"My mentioning intellect here is to introduce its connection to metaphysical function. Intellect relates to the metaphysical but no human's intellect comprehends the metaphysical – no layperson's intellect, no historian's, no scholar's, no theologian's, no scientist's. The most abstract or profound thought can merely conjecture or conceptualize - not understand, comprehend or 'know' the metaphysical or its functionary – however/whatever that may be.

Intellect came to the human species over hundreds of thousands of years. Intelligent actions gradually, oh so slowly, replaced instinctual reactions. The first (seminal) evidence of human intelligence had to be the recognition that others of the human species also had intelligence.

This approach brings me to the conceptualization that compassion (being responsible to/with fellow humans) was the first purpose for life discovered by the human and religious beliefs (being response-able to some metaphysical functionary) came eons later."

Compassion had to exist then, within emerging human life, otherwise the human animal could not have survived to the point in time of recognizing that it is response–able to the metaphysical functionary. Compassion has to exist now, and henceforth, if the human is to survive its weapons (nuclear and biological) and its destructive practices (vs: climate and natural resources).

This blog could end here and the point I set out to make would have been presented. But the reader surely knows that a weakness of those who write is to write on - even after the intended thought has been delivered.

Hominid remains, artifacts and accurate dating methods present expanding evidence that the evolution of Homo sapiens has not been a smooth, trouble free continuum. One does not have to delve too far into the relationship of the Neanderthal and Homo sapiens strains of the human to become aware of a profound mystery. Why did Neanderthal disappear and Homo sapiens emerge?

I am not an anthropologist or paleontologist nor capable of related conclusions. Even my extensive reading in this area has been for informational fulfillment and not to claim expertise. I wondered if there was some adequate explanation of the Neanderthal mystery to lend credence to my conjecture that metaphysical information via responsible compassion came to the human prior to metaphysical information via response-able religion.

Accurate sources reveal that the Neanderthal actually had greater brain size than Homo sapiens. Other studies attempt to determine if the factor was habitat (ice ages, etc.) but to little avail. One theory offers the vague supposition that Homo sapiens recognized the "benefits" of religion to greater depth than Neanderthal, hence attaining survival. My current supposition would substitute the word compassion for religion in the previous sentence and I would offer that by whatever means, and from whence it came, compassion was the edge for Homo sapiens.

I would suggest the reader go to the web and read just a few of the thousands of articles available on the Neanderthal vs. Homo sapiens mystery and then join me, not in the impossible – solving the mystery – but in the hopeful - trying to be living proof that Homo sapiens is both responsible to all of humanity and response-able to the greatest mystery of all, the metaphysical "information," the nudge, the atmosphere of possibilities, the Incomprehensible God of the Universe.

My theory that the survival trait of compassion evolved in the human ahead of the developed trait of religion is, of course, open to strenuous discussion; but I state that it did and I rest my case.

There is another question that arises on this side of the prehistoric. Is the trait of religion best defined by the adjective compassionate or passionate? That is where the next blog will be directed.

But wait! This morning's mail brought a copy of Bishop John Shelby Spong's latest book, "Eternal Life: A New Vision."

So – instead of working on a new blog this week, I shall read his book and share my critique of it prior to dealing with compassionate vs. passionate, as in religion.

15. Discovered: The Self Consciousness Link

The complete title of Bishop Spong's latest book is:
"Eternal Life: A New Vision (Beyond Religion, Beyond Theism, Beyond Heaven and Hell)"

Some books are serendipitous. Earlier in this blog series I described a friend loaning me the book "Genes, Genesis and God, Their Origins in Natural and Human History," by Holmes Rolston III.

In the book I found the following quote (p.367).

"The divine spirit is the giver of life, pervasively present over the millennia. God is the atmosphere of possibilities, the metaphysical environment, in, with, and under first the natural and later also the cultural environment, luring the Earthen histories upslope."

Dr. Rolston loaned me the metaphor, "God is the atmosphere of possibilities."

In this series of blogs I have been struggling with the infusion into life of, first, value and then purpose. In a lifeless world I reasoned that the appearance of life gave value. I concluded that true purpose came into life when the human evolved from instinctual reaction to intelligent action. I used "intelligent action" as a marker. Now I find another serendipitous book. In his latest book Bishop Spong has loaned me a much better marker that I shall borrow for the future – "self consciousness."

The first few chapters of the book are autobiographical in describing how John Shelby Spong the child came to be Bishop Spong, a proficient professional within Christian Religion. Several chapters then reveal the transformation of his personal belief system from that established by traditional religion over its centuries to his present one evolved through his experiential lifetime. The concluding chapters describe how liberated persons can have new visions beyond the restrictions of religion, theism, heaven and hell.

My four score + years match his described by Bishop Spong so that "me too" was my response to his observations. Elinor and I live in a retirement community with octogenarians who frequently exhale "we too" as experiential agreements. What amazes me is how accomplished many of my peers are at pretending that they believe what traditional religion tells them they should believe when they actually struggle with humankind's innate doubts.

One of my best friends uses these words to describe those who take their religion "too seriously." – "Way down deep he/she is really very shallow."

This may be true with some but I am finding that with most of my peers - if you dig deep enough you will find them "really very deep." They simply find it easier to appear to accept the shallowness of traditional religion than to explain to the establishment that it is easier to pretend than protest.

It is my conclusion that Bishop Spong's new book is a good read for Seniors, because at our age we have "been there - pondered that." I grasp his term "self consciousness." Since I do not know what he means by the term "mystical experience," I'll defer on that one.

16. Compassionate or Passionate?

In a previous book, "A Belief System from Beyond the Box" I arrived at a one sentence statement of my beliefs.

"I believe that the Incomprehensible God of the Universe is an Atmosphere of Possibilities within which the human can be a response-able steward to and for the Incomprehensible God – and responsible to and with all of humanity, including self."

In that statement I touch on two relationships vital to the human: as a response-able steward to and for God and as a fellow human responsible to and with all of humanity. Some may say, "What about the human's relationship with the Universe and with all other life on the Earth?" I would see this question answered by the declaration that the human has evolved to the level of being the Incomprehensible God's steward for our tiny speck of the universe and for all other life within that microcosm.

A foreboding aside:

Teilhard de Chardin said, "Man has grabbed the tiller of the world." Some will, and some will not, agree with that statement. But I will make a statement that is far too similar and far too true, "Man has become capable of disabling the tiller of the world." e.g. Nuclear and biological weapons, climate change and destruction of resources.

These, then, are the relationships of the human. What are the preeminent traits of the human? We can find them in millions of writings but we need go no further than Paul's First Letter to the Corinthians, Chapter 13.

"So faith, hope, love abide, these three; but the greatest of these is love."

Often we are prone to attempt rendering our observations so simple that we make them simplistic. Of course there are other eminent human traits; honest, trustworthy, charitable ... but if we love and are worthy of being loved all other traits are subsets. What should we bring to our relationships (with humans, the universe, Nature, God) other than love? **But - can we bring love without bringing compassion?**

Although many humans try, I cannot bring myself to believe that the myriad wonders that do and will exist could be accidental. In my inadequate way in "Blog 14. Discovered – the Compassionate Link," I conjectured that there is something beyond the physical, the "informational nudge" from the metaphysical, which we humans cannot comprehend. Although I do not know what the "nudge" is, I am convinced that Compassion has to be a part of the process.

As the Universe is expanding and life is evolving, God, as the Atmosphere of Possibilities, is expanding and evolving.

As the previous sentence courses onto my computer's screen, I am reminded of the book, "The Evolution of God," Little, Brown & Company, © 2009, by Robert Wright who traces the stages of human development (hunter-gatherer, agrarian, etc.) and via the religions developed by humans within those stages on into subsequent faith systems (Buddhist, Hindu, Judeo-Christian, Islam, etc.).

Is Wright's book a delineation of the evolution of God or a delineation of the evolution of God religions?

If we stretch our thoughts beyond the physical to a metaphysical Atmosphere of Evolving Possibilities could we then speak in terms of the evolution of God?

To date I have only read a lengthy introduction to Wright's book. When I have completed the book I shall devote a blog or two to my reaction as a layperson.

For now I shall return to the subject at hand.

Does too much passion for any religion, as compared to the passion of others for their religions, deter the evolution of mutual compassion? History and experience say yes.

Does too much passion for our specific, definitive religion result in our taking our religion too seriously? History and experience say yes.

17. Compassion (Teeter) vs. Passion (Totter)

Why would I use the metaphor of a teeter-totter, usually considered playground equipment, to compare serious terms like compassion and passion? Why? Because I so often find myself, and my peers, being on that teeter-totter.

In my defense I will say that I consider totter the more unsteady of the two terms and I reserve it for the emotion I consider the less stable of the two, passion. I find compassion, as teeter, the more difficult to come by, but the more stable when achieved.

Research and subsequent volumes of articles and books have been devoted to studies of the emotive conditions, passion and compassion. This is not my area of expertise, but like anyone studying a subject, I could regurgitate page upon page of hyperbole dressing that topic in the emperor's new clothes (e.g. sort of a home-spun theology). But I won't.

The fabric I shall weave will be a swatch of life. The warp will be the life of W. W. Watson and the weft will be life in the Great Depression.

How many readers remember October 29, 1929? Not many – but I shall claim to be one.

One would guess that not a single person in New Philadelphia, Indiana owned shares of stock affected by the Black Friday Market Crash of October 29, 1929. But they would be wrong. My Grandmother Wiggs owned some stock in a Cleveland, Ohio Cemetery, and her son-in-law, my father, owned a like amount. How did they come by this stock?

In the heydays before 1929 it was common practice for stock shares salesmen to travel rural America stopping at general stores and progressive looking farms to ply their sometimes, questionable trade. A pair of these travelers made such a good presentation of how providing a final resting place for the deceased of Cleveland, Ohio would be to their eternal edification AND increased wealth of my grandmother and father – that they bought in. My mother always said it was a gift of providence that they both bit because the same house could not have accommodated the extended family if only one had erred in becoming a gullible, venture capitalist.

Any amount was a large amount, in those days, so there was a second blessing within the story. It was - how many years it took for the stock to become utterly worthless – that being much later and in better times.

But I digress.

During the Great Depression property was very cheap in Southern Indiana. People who salvaged anything from a former affluence could purchase shelter and some ground there on which to scratch out a living.

W. W. Watson moved into the old Jones place one-mile East of New Philadelphia. He came from Chicago. He had no wife. He had two sons in their early teens. He professed no political connection nor discussed the same. He ventured no interest in any religious institution nor discussed the same.

And thus the rumors flew. Was he from Cicero? Could he be Polish (He talked differently from Hoosiers.) Was his real name

Watsoniski? Was he a former gangster? There were no Catholics in Franklin Township. Could he be one? On and on and on . . .

But let me tell the "rest of the story." W.W. was a most compassionate neighbor. He helped anytime there was a need. He worked hard. He and his sons were neat in appearance, in speech and in attitude. They always paid their bills. The sons were good students. The family's only visible deficit was no connection to a church in this semi-Bible-belt community.

The rural churches of the community regularly held "Revivals." A preacher from somewhere else was always the "Revivalist." These two- week events drew nightly crowds from throughout the county and even from beyond. During the early 1930s such a revival was in full swing at the Methodist Church in New Philadelphia. One night, for some reason never discovered, W.W. Watson, who never attended church, was present in a pew at the rear of the church. Nearer the front was a middle-aged woman, an unknown to any of the locals, a vocally enthusiastic participant. At an appropriate moment for testimonials she rose and proclaimed, "I'm married to the Lord." Later she rose and doubled her testimony, "I'm married, I'm married to the Lord." Witnesses stated that W. W appeared to grow nervous at these words. Still a third time she pronounced in triplicate, " I'm married, I'm married, I'm married to the Lord."

This time W. W. could contain himself no longer and he rose and responded, "Lady, I don't know your background but I will say one thing. You married into a damn good family."

Thus W. W. Watson became a permanent part of the anecdotal history of religion in New Philadelphia, Franklin Township, Washington County, Southern Indiana.

When better times returned, W. W. sold the "Old Jones Place, much improved and now referred to as the "Watson Place." Rumors flowed again. This time rumor described W. W. as a mechanical engineer, his old job in industry had opened up in Chicago and they were returning so the sons could pursue college careers.

Over the years I have considered the incongruities in this revival story. A negative position: Why was W. W. present that night? Had he been drinking?

A positive position: Had he finally reached the limit of his patience with a religious system too passionate for his compassionate nature?

Within my limited knowledge as a boy but more importantly through the adults in my life there was never a doubting whisper concerning W. W. and abstinence. Therefore I long ago tossed out the negative position.

How then to explain the positive position?

Over the years I have concluded that W. W. Watson was ahead of compassion's curve* in a community where too many took their religious belief systems too seriously (too passionately).

* In an address made to the Tenth Anniversary Convention of the Southern Christian Leadership Conference in Atlanta on August 16, 1967, Dr. Martin Luther King stated: "Let us realize the **arc** of the moral universe is long, but it bends towards **justice**."

In the present era a paraphrase of this truth gives us hope -

"Let us realize the **arc** of the religious universe is long, but it bends towards **compassion**."

18. The Arc of the Religious Universe

It is certainly true that the arc of the religious universe is long, in time and in dimension. Since it's ancient emergence within human history, religion has spread to involve the entire human species. Archeology indicates that the first bending of religion was toward the hope for an extended existence through some sort of eternal life. Later theories (actually suppositions, e.g. Neanderthals vs. Homo sapiens) would indicate a bending toward hope for compassionate relationships between humans.

This ethic has been present in all religions and writings thereof since earliest known times. This bending of religion toward compassion has come to be known as, "The Golden Rule," a.k.a. "The Ethics of Reciprocity," or "Reciprocal Altruism." (Earlier I suggested the rather long-winded description, "The Rule for Universal

Human Compassion." I doubt if tradition will rush to accept this definition.)

All religions claim adherence to the Ethic of Reciprocity within some context. There is also a tendency for religions to claim (at least indicate) that compassion has evolved from, or through, religion. However there is manifold evidence that passion was a part of human nature (e.g. the biological process, the genetic pool) long before there was human religion. Thus there is every indication that compassion, which is a kinship extension of passion, is of a secular and not a religious origin and was present in the human biological make-up, the genetic pool, long before religion came to the human scene. If readers are internet equipped they should go to the following website:

http://www.ted.com/talks/robert_wright_the_evolution_of_compassion.html

and spend a valuable 16 minutes and 57 seconds viewing Robert Wright (Author of "The Evolution of God") in a marvelous dissertation supporting this thesis. This video is so easy to view and so germane to the evolution of compassion that I shall make no attempt to transpose/translate it into the form of this blog.

In addition it is so easy to use a search engine aimed at "Robert Wright on Compassion" that I will make no attempt to interpret for him. Of course the precepts of contrarians abound. Even though I disagree with them I heartily encourage the reader to search them out on his/her own to obtain an objective view - a view confirming that compassion is a part of humanity's inherent nature and was present before religion emerged.

I constantly remind myself, and hence the reader, that our purpose is to determine if humans are prone to take their specific religions too passionately and seriously, thus depriving the total humanity of compassionate kinship.

In that light, in the next blog, I shall revisit the brief moment in the life of W. W. Watson that earned him everlasting, anecdotal significance in New Philadelphia, Indiana (at least in my cache of memorable anecdotes).

19. A Memoir for an Anecdote.

Before I present a memoir portraying the W. W. Watson anecdote mentioned in a previous blog, [17. Compassion (Teeter) vs. Passion (Totter)] I need to elaborate on the significance of anecdotes in my nurturing community. In that day, in that rural society, individuals came to be stereotyped by actions and words that attained anecdotal status.

Thus W. W. Watson came to be known as, "The fellow who responded at a revival to that holy-roller, outlander woman who claimed she was married to the Lord." This identification would be followed by a glee-filled quoting of W. W.'s punch line; "But I will say one thing, you married into a damn good family." For years after the Watson family left the community, if their name, or a reference to their farm, came up in the loafing crowd at the general store this anecdote was a sure bet to once again receive full disclosure.

I still remember the discussion at our family supper-table the evening after the actual event. My father told the story in such a manner that one could easily sense his support of Mr. Watson. My Grandmother did not support public displays of religious passion but she disapproved even more of appearing to make fun of those who chose to do so. My mother struggled to remain neutral. My sisters knew better than to giggle and I was too young to have an opinion. I also remember that the incident did not become a teaching moment.

Years later when I was an adult the Watson anecdote came up in a discussion with my father. I asked him why he thought Mr. Watkins went out of character in his response that night. Dad said it had always been his evaluation that Mr. Watson had not intended to insult the lady but had reached his limit of endurance with revivals and folks taking religion **too** seriously. My father offered this conclusion, "Religion is serious stuff so we must be careful not to hurt ourselves, or harm others, with it."

20. Religion <u>Is</u> Serious Stuff.

This is, of course, an understatement. However, when coupled within the observation, "Religion is serious stuff which can be hurtful and harmful when taken too seriously," it becomes a beneficial statement of reality.

But - it is so easy for us to determine when others are taking **their** religion too seriously. It is so difficult for us to determine when we are taking **our** religion too seriously.

I'm sure the passionate lady at the revival had no intention of affronting anyone's level of compassion. In fact many in attendance would have responded, "Amen," to her pronouncement. A far lesser number, in this audience, would have supported Mr. Watson in his reaction.

Religion was so serious to this passionate lady that she had to frame her relationship with God in terms of the deepest human relationship she could comprehend: husband – wife. Did she mean she was married to God as Lord or to Christ as Lord? (At no revival in my experience did a man proclaim that he was married to the Lord. However, several times at revivals I have learned that God, especially as Christ, was a "Bosom Buddy" of men where one would never have suspected such a strong relationship.)

Others claim God as a father relationship: father -- son, father – daughter. There is Christ as a brother to brother relationship and Christ as brother to sister. Is it not strange that the anthropomorphically inclined human ignores the strongest bond of all: mother – child, within this societal universe that bends so sharply toward the patriarchal definition of God?

Finally within my revival exposures there were always those in attendance "filled" with the Holy Spirit. (Traditionally that Holy Spirit was a male.)

Can passion mislead individuals to apply their religion "too seriously". . . . and "selfishly?" Does compassion lead individuals to utilize their religion "practically" and ". . . . . . mutually?"

Do we define "too seriously?" per our discernment? per our perception?

21. Discernment or Perception?

This blog is going to deal with the meanings of "discernment" and "perception." These words have many meanings as found in dictionaries: Here are a couple.

discernment – (In Christian contexts) - Perception in the absence of judgment with a view to obtaining spiritual direction and understanding.

perception – a way of regarding, understanding, or interpreting something – a mental impression.

This blog is also going to approach these words from an "experiential perspective."

experiential – involving or based on experience or observation.

My exposures to revivals came at a time in my early life when I did not qualify as capable of discerning or perceiving the authenticity of other persons' expressions of their religious practices. It is just as well that my experiential reporting of "too seriously" be from illustrations other than my exposures to revivals.

None of those present at the "I'm married to the Lord" episode could speak to the "too seriously" dilemma because the lady was an unknown. Thus discernment and perception were to no avail. As I've reported, neighbors did step forward to defend Mr. Watson. But they would be termed "prejudicial witnesses" in any attempt to assign compassion as his motivation. Again a revival setting fails the test of objectivity.

Over many years in the same community, I observed one characteristic practiced by some that I came to consider as "taking one's religion seriously."

Jacob (this was not his real name) carried his leather-covered Bible at all times. During usual Wednesday night or Sunday church hours he was dressed in suit, shirt, tie in a fashion that he could step into any church service that he came upon.

I am going to state from the outset of my description of Jacob that I am not belittling his life style or his beliefs. Jacob and I did not attend the same church but we were casual friends. We could discuss anything from nature to politics to religion – not always agreeing.

Janie (this was not her real name) carried her leather–covered bible at all times. She attended every funeral held in our community, irregardless of the denomination.

I am going to state from the outset of my description of Janie that I am not belittling her life style or her beliefs. Janie and I did not attend the same church but we were "greet when you meet on the street" friends. Our meetings did not involve discussions.

It would be my perception that I considered both Jacob and Janie as displaying eccentricities within their religious practices. However because I could discern Jacob more accurately than I could discern Janie I rated his mannerisms as "serious" and hers I rated as "too serious."

It must be noted that my experiential perspectives had been conditioned to include the "judgment" that those who attend funerals indiscriminately are somehow taking religion too seriously. Thus my perceptions of Janie's religious practices were distorted and my discernments of Jacob's practices were merely skewed.

As we search for examples of persons taking religion too seriously, I trust that we are aware of the acquired conditionings that too often lurk in our minds . . . . **as we behold our fellow humans' "too serious" transgressions.**

22. A Functional Molecule

In the previous blog I recognized that we distort our perceptions and discernments of others and of their actions by inserting our personal conditionings, as biased judgments, into our appraisals. How do we acquire these conditionings?

Family, community, school, society, vocations, media, governments (local, national, global), etc. - and let us not forget the most important etc. of all – our religions.

Religions try diligently to prove that they are not errant.

Religions try even more prodigiously to prove that they are inerrant.

If the religion is a book religion it applies the same principles to its book.

Religions are expert at conditioning minds. They use manipulations that I have dubbed "innocent errancy."

> **innocent-errancy** – a coined term to express the state of believing errant information innocently because it is the best explanation currently available. e.g. The world is flat (1491), the Biblical creation stories, the early concept that the Sun rotated around the Earth, God could make the sun stand still.

Christians need to read only 25 verses into their Judeo-Christian Bible until they come to the ultimate innocent-errancy:
Genesis 1: 26-27 (KJV)

> And God said, Let us make man in our image, after our likeness: and let them have dominion over the fish of the sea, and over the fowl of the air, and over the cattle, and over all the earth, and over every creeping thing that creepeth upon the earth. 27 So God created man in his own image, in the image of God created he him; male and female created he them.

Thus one can say Biblically, "I'm created, created in the image of God." But like the woman at the revival who proclaimed, "I'm married, married to the Lord," this would be taking one's religion too seriously.

Recently one of my dearest friends, with whom I exchange deepest thoughts, sent me an e-mail in which he used a quote from Thomas Merton to make a point. Here is the e-mail:

I really appreciate the following Merton definition:

"To say that I am made in the image of God is to say that love is the reason for my existence, for God is love. Love is my true identity. Selflessness is my true self. Love is my true character. Love is my name."
        - Thomas Merton, from A Book of Hours

The Old Testament writer thought (knew?) that God is comprehensible and thus could state that God designed the comprehensible human as an image of God. It remained for a New Testament writer, a certain "elder," to write a letter to one of the churches under his general supervision and explain that God is comprehensible as love.

His statement in The First Letter of John, Chapter 4, Verses 7, 8 (RSV)

7 Beloved, let us love one another; for love is of God, and one who loves is born of God and knows God. 8 He who does not love does not know God; for God is love.

Merton knew that God is incomprehensible and the incomprehensible cannot be imaged. Yet his religious conditioning led him to predicate his relationship with God, and with his fellow humans, on the innocent-errancy that we are made in the image of the "non-'imageable' God, who is love." Hence -

"Love is my true identity. Selflessness is my true self. Love is my true character. Love is my name." Merton

The metaphor that "God is love" seemingly approaches Anselm's definition of God: "that than which nothing greater can be thought." But love as a metaphor can be so ambiguous and the "nothing greater" phrase can be so nebulous that both fall short of exactitude.

These deficiencies lend credence to Rolston's conception of God as the Atmosphere of Possibilities. One of those possibilities is to think of oneself as a barely detectable (though quite kinetic) molecule in that Atmosphere of Possibilities.

I would propose that this could sustain a healthy concept of human existence wherein one does not take oneself too seriously.

23. Happy As a Kinetic Molecule.

Genesis 1-27. So God created man in his own image, in the image of God created he him; male and female created he them.

This verse has to be the bedrock statement of all theological statements.

> A specific dictionary states:
> A theologian is a person who engages or is an expert in theology.
> And:
> Theology is the study of the nature of God and religious belief.

Thus, in keeping with Biblical theology:

All male and female theologians, created in the image of the one God, will therefore report a uniform description of the nature of God and religious belief.
(Nope. It doesn't seem to turn out that way.)

I went to the search engine Google and asked for - Theologians?

Here is the address I was given:

http://www.theology.ie/theologs.htm

When I called up the address - how fortunate, I had at my fingertips the 71 (seventy-one!) theologians of the world. I had no idea there were so few. I was thrilled that my research would be so limited. But alas –
I started with Abelard (first on the list).

I struggled through his travails of getting an education, of fathering a son only to have his wife leave him to go to a nunnery, of several imprisonments because of arguments with the religious authorities. He picked a fight with Anselm's students that did not turn out well. I shall quote the final two paragraphs of this internet biography: Peter Abelard (1079-1142)

"St. Bernard sums up the charges against Abelard when he writes (Ep. cxcii) "Cum de Trinitate loquitur, sapit Arium; cum do gratiâ, sapit Pelagium; cum de personâ Christi, sapit Nestorium", and there is no doubt that on these several heads Abelard wrote and said many things which were open to objection from the point of view of orthodoxy. That is to say, while combating the opposite errors, he fell inadvertently into mistakes which he himself did not recognize as Arianism, Pelagianism, and Nestorianism, and which even his enemies could characterize merely as savouring of Arianism, Pelagianism, and Nestorianism. Abelard's influence on his immediate successors was not very great, owing partly to his conflict with the ecclesiastical authorities, and partly to his personal defects, more especially his vanity and pride, which must have given the impression that he valued truth less than victory.

His influence on the philosophers and theologians of the thirteenth century was, however, very great. It was exercised chiefly through Peter Lombard, his pupil, and other framers of the "Sentences." Indeed, while one must be careful to discount the exaggerated encomiums of Compayré, Cousin, and others, who represent Abelard as the first modern, the founder of the University of Paris, etc., one is justified in regarding him, in spite of his faults of character and mistakes of judgment, as an important contributor to scholastic method, an enlightened opponent of obscurantism, and a continuator of that revival of learning which occurred in the Carolingian age, and of which whatever there is of science, literature, and speculation in the early Middle Ages is the historical development."

I was sorry that he got all tangled up in Arianism, Pelagianism, and Nestorianism but it was a relief to learn "His influence on the philosophers and theologians of the thirteenth century was, however, very great."

I then turned to the second theologian on the list, Albert the Great a.k.a. St. Albertus the Magnus. This was a different story. His biography was solid 24-karat platitudes. I am convinced that his only transgression was going to bed one time when he was seven without brushing his teeth. I shall copy here the section on his theology.

Albert's theology

In theology Albert occupies a place between Peter Lombard, the Master of the Sentences, and St. Thomas Aquinas. In systematic order, in accuracy and clearness he surpasses the former, but is inferior to his own illustrious disciple. His "Summa Theologiae" marks an advance beyond the custom of his time in the scientific order observed, in the elimination of useless questions, in the limitation of arguments and objections; there still remain, however, many of the *impedimenta*, hindrances, or stumbling blocks, which St. Thomas considered serious enough to call for a new manual of theology for the use of beginners — *ad eruditionem incipientium*, as the Angelic Doctor modestly remarks in the prologue of his immortal "Summa". The mind of the *Doctor Universalis* was so filled with the knowledge of many things that he could not always adapt his expositions of the truth to the capacity of novices in the science of theology. He trained and directed a pupil who gave the world a concise, clear, and perfect scientific exposition and defence of Christian Doctrine; under God, therefore, we owe to Albertus Magnus the "Summa Theologica" of St. Thomas.

At this point in my research I was relieved to learn that St. Thomas Aquinas in his "Summa Theologica" had given the world a "concise, clear and *perfect* [blog author's italics] scientific exposition and defense of Christian Doctrine" and there would be no need for me to check out the other 69 (sixty-nine) theologians.

Someday I may be moved to read the *perfect* "Summa Theologica."

In the meantime I must remain content with my imperfect movements as a kinetic molecule in the Atmosphere of Possibilities.

24. Exactitude

It's happened again. Not since the time in a previous blog series when I changed the phrase from, "The Church must change or it will die," to the substitute, "The Church must morph to survive," have I been in such epistemological hot water. At that time one of my friends was sure that it was improper to reduce metamorphosis, a noun, to morph, a verb. Now another friend is sure that it is improper to expand exact, an adjective, to exactitude, a noun.

Here was the usage in Blog 22:

> "The metaphor that 'God is love' seemingly approaches Anselm's definition of God: 'that than which nothing greater can be thought.' But love as a metaphor can be so ambiguous and the 'nothing greater' phrase can be so nebulous that both fall short of exactitude."

At this writing we (my friend and I) are in the process of determining if my friend is objecting to word usage (exactitude) or concept presentation (here is the paragraph which followed).

> "These deficiencies lend credence to Rolston's conception of God as the Atmosphere of Possibilities. One of those possibilities is to think of oneself as a barely detectable (though quite kinetic) molecule in that Atmosphere of Possibilities."

After my experience with Abelard and Albertus Magnus, described in Blog 23, I am convinced that theologians and their biographers tend toward verbosity, plus – as an additional distraction – hyperbole.

"He [Albertus Magnus] trained and directed a pupil [St. Thomas Aquinas] who gave the world a concise, clear, and perfect scientific exposition and defence of Christian Doctrine; under God."

Periodically I read through my previous blogs to see what I said so I won't say it again. This is a practice within daily life which those of us living in retirement communities find helpful. However this time I found something that I want to say again in order to change the direction of this blog series. Here are the final three paragraphs of blog 12.

Anselm says the metaphysical functionary is God, a he with being which Anselm characterizes as "that than which nothing greater can be thought."

Seems to me, "that than which nothing greater can be thought," would be incomprehensible. How then do we comprehend that God is a he and is a being, and is greater than something else?

Tillich appears to be on much firmer ground (no pun) when he describes God as the "Ground of All Being."

I'll just tag along with the thought that the Metaphysical Functionary is the Incomprehensible God of the Universe luring earthen histories upslope – dressed appropriately for the occasion in the fabric of possibilities rather than unintelligible threads of hyperbole.

Sometimes writers find, or construct, phrases that influence them so thoroughly that they simply can't let go of them. I am that way with Holmes Roston III's likening the Incomprehensible God of the Universe to the Atmosphere of Possibilities luring earthen histories upslope.

I have for many years seen a remarkable synergism between many of the hyperbolic writings about religion and the story of the Emperor's new clothes. Thus when I couple Rolston's, "The Incomprehensible God is the Atmosphere of Possibilities luring earthen histories upslope," with my addition, "dressed appropriately for the occasion in the fabric of possibilities rather than unintelligible threads of hyperbole," I find myself the possessor of an infatuating concept.

How does this sentence change the direction of this blog series? My initial intent was to reveal examples of my peers taking their religious beliefs too seriously, even to the point of being harmful or hurtful to others. As I have explored the lives and theological beliefs of those identified as theologians I find them taking their theology too seriously, even to the point of being harmful or hurtful to others in centuries past and centuries present. Thus I would add a second purpose to this blog series, searching out illustrations of theologians who took/take theology too seriously, e.g. John Calvin, although he helped condemn Michael Servetus to death for heresy did try, at least, to redirect Servetus' death to beheading because it would be - "quicker and less painful" than burning at the stake.

Therefore I find myself obliged to add – "taking theology too seriously" - to my original concern – "taking religion too seriously." However, I shall temper the statement to a more respectful version – "taking theology too inappropriately."

25. Innocent-Errancy Revisited.

Here I shall restate some of the material from Blog 22, wherein I introduced the term *innocent-errancy*:

"Religions are expert at conditioning minds. They use a manipulation that I have dubbed the 'innocent errancy.'

> **innocent-errancy** – a coined term to express the state of believing errant information innocently because it is the best explanation currently available. e.g. The world is flat (1491), the Biblical creation stories, the early concept that the Sun rotated around the Earth, God could make the sun stand still.

Christians need to read only 25 verses into their Judeo-Christian Bible until they come to the ultimate innocent-errancy:

> Genesis 1: 26-27 (KJV)
> And God said, Let us make man in our image, after our likeness: and let them have dominion over the fish of the sea, and over the fowl of the air, and over the cattle, and over all the

earth, and over every creeping thing that creepeth upon the earth. 27 So God created man in his own image, in the image of God created he him; male and female created he them.

Thus the human could say, biblically, "I'm created, created in the image of God."

I would maintain that one is into theology inappropriately, perhaps perversely, if one bases her/his theology on the ultimate innocent-errancy, held adversely over the centuries as theological truth, e.g. the primitive concept that, "God created man in his own image." More and more authentic theological thought is coming to the realization that God is indefinable and incomprehensible. Yet too often variant theological thought "defines" God through anthropomorphic characteristics deriving from "created image man" and via noble human traits such as love and compassion. Even the term "theological thought" diminishes the incomprehensibility of God, because "theology" and "thought" are human constructs. "God is love," is also a human construct.

I went to an internet search engine and fed in – "God created man in his own image." I was presented 3,420,000 entries to choose from. I then fed in – "God is creating man in his own image." I was presented a mere 1,870,000 entries. I'm working on the latter list. I am on the verge of submitting this as entry 1,870,001:

"The Incomprehensible God is evolving the comprehensible human within an atmosphere of possibilities, saturated with compassion, that lures human history upslope."

Holmes Rolston III (Expanded via insertion of "saturated with compassion")

Although I am confidant that Mark Twain was not writing in exegetical terms, I feel that he was posing an accurate question when he penned this:
"It is said that man is the noblest work of God. Now I wonder – who found that out?"

If we were to join Anselm in concluding that the basic statement of theology is, "God is that than which nothing greater can be thought," and then join the writers of Genesis in the belief that "God created man in his own image," would these statements falsely define an incomprehensible, original God image as being represented by the comprehensible, facsimile human? Would this not be the ultimate innocent-errancy?

I fear that it would. No, I fear that it is -- if we try to follow the diverse courses of belief held by much of the Christian Faith.

26. Abelard Revisited

Earlier, in Blog 23, it was noted that the Biblical writers, through the ultimate innocent-errancy, state that all humans are created in the image of God. This would infer that all theologians, as images, would produce uniform descriptions of the nature of God.

Also, in Blog 23, I described my encounter with Abelard as the first in alphabetical order of a mere 71 theologians offered by a search engine in response to my entry, "Theologians?"

The biographer of Abelard in that review was not especially complimentary of Abelard's personality or his theology. This may indicate that one's later description is at the mercy of the describer. Here I repeat what St. Bernard, and Abelard's biographer, said in the next to last paragraph of that specific biography:

"St. Bernard sums up the charges against Abelard when he writes (Ep. cxcii) "Cum de Trinitate loquitur, sapit Arium; cum do gratiâ, sapit Pelagium; cum de personâ Christi, sapit Nestorium", and there is no doubt that on these several heads Abelard wrote and said many things which were open to objection from the point of view of orthodoxy. That is to say, while combating the opposite errors, he fell inadvertently into mistakes which he himself did not recognize as Arianism, Pelagianism, and Nestorianism, and which even his enemies could characterize merely as savouring of Arianism, Pelagianism, and Nestorianism. Abelard's influence on his immediate successors was not very great, owing partly to his conflict with the ecclesiastical authorities, and partly to his personal defects, more especially his vanity and pride, which must have given the impression that he valued truth less than victory."

But wait – in this following, last paragraph the biographer reverses himself:

"His influence on the philosophers and theologians of the thirteenth century was, however, very great. It was exercised chiefly through Peter Lombard, his pupil, and other framers of the "Sentences." Indeed, while one must be careful to discount the exaggerated encomiums[*] of Compayré, Cousin, and others, who represent Abelard as the first modern, the founder of the University of Paris, etc., one is justified in regarding him, in spite of his faults of character and mistakes of judgment, as an important contributor to scholastic method, an enlightened opponent of obscurantism, and a continuator of that revival of learning which occurred in the Carolingian age, and of which whatever there is of science, literature, and speculation in the early Middle Ages is the historical development."

What is the layperson to believe in the face of St. Bernard's Latin, which the typical layperson cannot translate, nor the terms, Arianism, Pelagianism, Nestorianism and Carolingian age which the average layperson has not studied?

It was my decision to learn more about Abelard. I found a biography of Abelard under the name Abailard in a book titled "Christian Doctrine Lectures" authored by Robert Lowry Calhoun, Copyright 1948, Yale Divinity School, New Haven Connecticut.

I discovered that Theologian Robert Calhoun had a very different view of Abailard than the other biographer had of Abelard. As I read Calhoun's 1948 work on Abailard I find the following quote at the bottom of page 286:

"Now, **if I seek to substantiate faith in God by appeal to reason,** it seems to Abailard that I may call attention to such considerations as these. It is necessary to regard God as the Ground of the existence of continuously existing things." (boldface added by blog author)

It is interesting to note that Paul Tillich later attracted attention within theological circles with the phrase, "God is the Ground of all being," in his volumes of "Systematic Theology," (1951-63).

Reading further in Calhoun I came to this quote at the top of page 287:

"It is necessary to regard [per Abailard] God as the purposeful and rational Designer of an ordered universe."

Again it is interesting to note that the term "Designer" used by Abailard (1079-1142) reappears in Creationist usage in the 21st Century as - "Intelligent Design."

When we ponder on the infinite theological premises that have been generated by the numbers of humans who have considered their creation to be in the image of God, it gives unlimited credence to the adage; "There is nothing new under the sun."

[*] encomium – noun (pl. –miums or –mia) formal a speech or piece of writing that praises someone or something highly.

27. More About Encomiums

Over the years my belief system has morphed. This system has moved slowly, but persistently, away from an acceptance of a Comprehensible God developed within climates of cultures toward a search for the Incomprehensible God shrouded in an Atmosphere of Possibilities.

Over the same span my conceptualization of theology and theologians has moved from inhibiting dependence to uninhibited release. I respect the need for an understanding of the nature of God. I respect theology. I respect those who devote their energies to seeking this understanding. I respect theologians. My conundrum is this: If the nature of God is assumed to be loving and universally fair, even as we realize that God is incomprehensible, how can one human's description of God's nature be more accurate than that of another human, based only on assumption?

Why should Anselm and Abelard, in past centuries, have greater or more valuable insights into the nature of God than extant humans in this century? Even further – Why should theologians who have studied every extinct and extant theological thought of all time have greater insight into **my** response-able relationship with God than I do? I need and welcome insights from many sources for consideration but I cannot possibly utilize all their diversity in my unique response-able relationship with God.

As an exercise in dealing with this dilemma let's sneak a quick look at three isms that Abelard supposedly flirted with -- much to the displeasure of his detractors:

Arianism, Pelagianism and Nestorianism. (Not household terms in my circle of theology seekers.)

"Arianism is defined as those teachings attributed to Arius which are in contrast to the current mainstream Trinitarian Christological dogma, as currently maintained by the Roman Catholic Church, the Eastern Orthodox Churches and many Protestant Churches. The term "Arianism" is also used to refer to other nontrinitarian theological systems of the 4th century, which regarded the Christ, Son of God, the Logos, as a created being (as in Arianism proper and Anomoeanism) or as neither uncreated nor created in the sense other beings are created (as in "Semi-Arianism")." [Wikipedia]

"*Pelagianism* is a theological theory named after Pelagius (AD 354 – AD 420/440), although ironically he denied, at least at some point in his life, many of the doctrines associated with his name. It is the belief that original sin did not taint human nature and that mortal will is still capable of choosing good or evil without special Divine aid." [Wikipedia]

"*Nestorianism* is the Christian doctrine that Jesus existed as two persons, the man Jesus and the divine Son of God, or Logos, rather than as a unified person. This doctrine is identified with Nestorius

(c. 386–c. 451), Patriarch of Constantinople. This view of Christ was condemned at the Council of Ephesus in 431, and the conflict over this view led to the Nestorian Schism, separating the Assyrian Church of the East from the Byzantine Church." [Wikipedia]

Arianism – Abelard would still fail the entrance exams for most Christian churches today if it were whispered that he was flirting with Arianism, Anomeanism, Semi Arianism or any other non-trinity theological system.

Pelagianism -- How to overcome Original Sin is not a big part of today's litmus test for Christian Church Membership, but the concept is still in force in many churches and Abelard (then) or John Doe (now) should check -- __x__ a. Special Divine Aid -- in response to the question -- "The only way to overcome original sin is?"

Nestorianism -- Here is the question:
Is Jesus, a. ___ The Divine Son of God? or, b. ___ The Ultimately Response-Able human?
Abelard (then) or John Doe (now) fails the test unless he checks:
a. ___

I do not make light of theology but as I believe beyond the boxes containing the "ABCS of the Comprehensible God of the Bible Verse" to the Incomprehensible God of the Universe, the Atmosphere of Possibilities." I must call box upon box of two thousand years of theology into question. Why?

In the realm of theology when a theologian comes upon a premise, be it sound or be it innocent-errancy, if enough supportive encomiums sprout - the premise flowers. If insufficient encomiums bud, the premise withers.

To those who are, and to those who are not, theologians, I say – we should be extremely careful which theological premises we endorse with our encomiums – lest they bloom and consume us in their innocent-errancy (i.e. "taking theology inappropriately").

28. Times Have Changed.

If the human cannot comprehend God (which I can't), but "hopes" that the nature of God is love, (which I do), how could that God permit (a theist phrase) the persecution or execution of one human for criticizing Christian dogma generated by other humans? I'll yield to theist thought to wrestle with that dilemma.

1. A historic example of persecution.
I am not in a position to defend Peter Abelard, about whom one biographer said this:

"Abelard's influence on his immediate successors was not very great, owing partly to his conflict with the ecclesiastical authorities, and partly to his personal defects, more especially his vanity and pride, which must have given the impression that he valued truth less than victory."

Apparently some religious authorities concluded that "vanity and pride" were grounds for Abelard's periodic persecution in the 12th Century. On that basis many of us in the 21st Century had better have an, "Oops, sorry" handy when we pronounce some of our statements.

But another biographer said quite the opposite about Abelard in what could be termed an encomium. What is one to deduce about a 12th Century theologian now in 2010?

2. A historic example of execution.
From many potential examples I have chosen the following, famous one from the 16th Century.

John Calvin was in a power struggle with the Geneva Council in July, 1553 and it appeared that his position would be lost. On August 13, 1553 Michael Servetus, a fugitive from ecclesiastical authorities, appeared in Geneva. Calvin and Servetus had carried on a long correspondence (thirty letters) as a theological debate (apparently about the Trinity) that had ended in Calvin's threat that, "If Servetus ever appears in Geneva, he will not leave alive." Calvin's turning Servetus in to the authorities was a turning point of Calvin's fortunes with the Council. Although Calvin requested the execution of Servetus (which the Council directed be, "slow burning at the stake,") he later asked that it be beheading as quicker and less painful. The execution was carried out as burning. [Condensed from Wikipedia]

It would appear to one in this 21ˢᵗ Century that a 16ᵗʰ Century dispute over the Trinity, ending in a burning at the stake, was, "taking theology far too inappropriately."

Human history is rife with tragedies related to religion:

Servetus (and many others), Crusades, Inquisitions, Genocides, The Witchcraft Trials, The Mormon "Massacres," The Holocaust, The "Davidian Massacre," The Jonestown Suicides, Terrorism, Attacks on Individuals, Groups or Masses, on and on and on.

And now -- Suicide Terrorism is in the news almost daily.

I do not trust my personal insights to understand nor explain the causes of suicidal terrorism. As I read descriptions in the media and dissertations by experts, I am increasingly aware that there can be no simple or direct, causal explanation of these horrific events. As I go to the media and to scholarly sources for information through which I can begin to understand why humans commit such perverse atrocities, I realize what a complicated, psychological, sociological, theological, pathological, tribal, nationalistic, horrific act this is. What internal torment or external conditioning could destroy so completely the compassionate and responsible behavior of one human and his/her abettors - "handlers" is a term used currently.

As I have searched current sources for an explanation, I believe that I have found one that can be termed reliable per the following quote:

"Dying to Win: The Strategic Logic of Suicide Terrorism (2005; ISBN 1-4000-6317-5) is Robert Pape's analysis of suicide terrorism from a strategic, social, and psychological point of view. It is based on a database he has compiled at the University of Chicago, where he directs the Chicago Project on Suicide Terrorism. The book's conclusions are based on data from 315 suicide terrorism campaigns around the world from 1980 through 2003 and 462 individual suicide terrorists. Published in May 2005, Pape's volume has been widely noticed by the press, the public, and policymakers alike, and has earned praise from the likes of Peter Bergen, Congressman Ron Paul (R-Texas), Michael Scheuer, and Noam Chomsky.

Dying to Win is divided into three parts, analyzing the strategic, social, and psychological dimension of suicide terrorism."

I would suggest that the reader go to the following url address: http://en.wikipedia.org/wiki/Dying_to_Win#Ch._2:_Explaining_Suicide_Terrorism

At that website under Contents is a summarization of Chapter 2.
1.1.2 Ch. 2: Explaining Suicide Terrorism
Here are the final sentences of that summarization:
"Traditional explanations focus on individual motives, but fail to explain the specificity of suicide terrorism (16-17). Economic explanation of this phenomenon yields "poor" results (17-19). Explanation of suicide terrorism as a form of competition between radical groups is dubious (19-20). Pape proposes an alternative explanation of the "causal logic of suicide terrorism": at the strategic level, suicide terrorism exerts coercive power against democratic states to cease occupation of territory terrorists consider homeland, while at the social level it depends on mass support and at the individual level it is motivated by altruism (20-23). "The bottom line, then, is that suicide terrorism is mainly a response to foreign occupation" (23).

I still remain incapable of understanding the motivation that triggers suicide terrorism. The question remains for me – Is the "motivating altruism," see above, based in nationalism or religion or . . . ? How is such a horrific personal conviction and act generated?

29. Is Wikipedia Reliable?

I knew it was coming. One of my most supportive readers amongst the uninhibited has sent an e-mail asking if I feel comfortable using Wikipedia frequently as a reference. Actually - many times I start with Wikipedia but branch out into other sources suggested by the original site. Other times I bypass Wikipedia and select other sources directly from a search engine such as Google or Yahoo.

As I prepared to answer my friend's query, I took a direct approach and fed the following question into Google. "Is Wikipedia reliable?"

The Number 1 source offered in a list, "of about 165,000" available, was this:

Is Wikipedia Reliable? - For Dummies.

I quite frequently read material published in print or electronically for "Dummies" so I did not take umbrage at being addressed, "For Dummies."

Here follows the website answer to the question:

Is Wikipedia Reliable?

The creators of Wikipedia are the first to admit that not every entry is accurate and that it might not be the best source of material for research papers. Here are some points to consider:
• **Look for a slant.** Some articles are fair and balanced, but others look more like the Leaning Tower of Pisa. If an article has only one source, beware.
• **Consider the source.** Even if an article cites external sources, check out those sources to see whether they are being cited fairly and accurately — and do, in fact, reinforce the article's points.
• **Look who's talking.** If you research the contributors themselves and find that they are experts in their fields, you can be more confident in the entry.
• **Start here, but keep going.** Wikipedia should be a starting point for research but not your primary source for research material.
In December 2005, the scientific journal *Nature* published the results of a study comparing the accuracy of Wikipedia and the printed Encyclopaedia Britannica. The researchers found that the number of "factual errors, omissions or misleading statements" in each reference work was not so different — Wikipedia contained 162, and Britannica

had 123. The makers of Britannica have since called on *Nature* to retract the study, which it claims is "completely without merit."

When visiting controversial entries, look out for *edit wars*. Edit wars occur when two contributors (or groups of contributors) repeatedly edit one another's work based on a particular bias. In early 2004, Wikipedia's founders organized an Arbitration Committee to settle such disputes.

Wikipedia does have some weaknesses that more traditional encyclopedias do not. For example

• There is no guarantee that important subjects are included or given the treatment that they deserve.

• Entries can be incomplete or in the middle of being updated at any given time.

• The writers of entries often fail to cite their original sources, thus making it hard to determine the credibility of the material.

These issues should not deter you from using Wikipedia. Just weigh the limitations of Wikipedia — and, for that matter, reference works in general.

Read more: http://www.dummies.com/how-to/content/is-wikipedia-reliable.html#ixzz0dBkEQXsh

---

I could ramble on in self defense but I shall rest my case by adding the following brief, personal encomium in behalf of Wikipedia and my use of its material.

This blog is written for the uninhibited layperson looking to morph her/his belief system in an effort to help the church morph so that it can survive. I am thankful that Wikipedia material, used in conjunction with limitless website material, is helpful in this task.

30. Posting Sad News

Wednesday, January 27, 2010 I posted blog #29 in the current series titled: "Is Wikipedia Reliable?"

For Wednesday, February 3, 2010 I was prepared to return to

posting material relative to the Charter for Compassion as obtained via e-mail and searched out using the web.

Thursday, January28 I tuned the TV at the usual 8:00 a.m. (after breakfast) to the independent, news program, "Democracy Now," hosted by Amy Goodman. The news started as routine and expected. President Obama had given his first State of the Union Address the night before.

But - the news was neither routine nor expected – Howard Zinn had died on Wednesday, January 27, 2010 from an apparent heart attack suffered while he was on vacation in Santa Monica, California. If the reader is aware of Howard Zinn's life this post dedicated to a review of his life will not come as a surprise. If the reader is not aware of the life of Howard Zinn this post will be not only be a surprise but an exposure to one of the most insightful minds present during recent years regarding America's past and present history.

I could research his life and add my observations but Columnist Bob Herbert has done this so effectively that I shall insert his excellent column from the January 30, 2010 New York Times as my tribute to the life of Howard Zinn.

January 30, 2010
OP-ED COLUMNIST
A Radical Treasure
By BOB HERBERT

I had lunch with Howard Zinn just a few weeks ago, and I've seldom had more fun while talking about so many matters that were unreservedly unpleasant: the sorry state of government and politics in the U.S., the tragic futility of our escalation in Afghanistan, the plight of working people in an economy rigged to benefit the rich and powerful.

Mr. Zinn could talk about all of that and more without losing his sense of humor. He was a historian with a big, engaging smile that seemed ever-present. His death this week at the age of 87 was a loss that should have drawn much more attention from a press corps that spends an inordinate amount of its time obsessing idiotically over the likes of Tiger Woods and John Edwards.

Mr. Zinn was chagrined by the present state of affairs, but undaunted. "If there is going to be change, real change," he said, "it will have to work its way from the bottom up, from the people themselves. That's how change happens."

We were in a restaurant at the Warwick Hotel in Manhattan. Also there was Anthony Arnove, who had worked closely with Mr. Zinn in recent years and had collaborated on his last major project, "The People Speak." It's a film in which well-known performers bring to life the inspirational words of everyday citizens whose struggles led to some of the most profound changes in the nation's history. Think of those who joined in — and in many cases became leaders of — the abolitionist movement, the labor movement, the civil rights movement, the feminist revolution, the gay rights movement, and so on.

Think of what this country would have been like if those ordinary people had never bothered to fight and sometimes die for what they believed in. Mr. Zinn refers to them as "the people who have given this country whatever liberty and democracy we have."

Our tendency is to give these true American heroes short shrift, just as we gave Howard Zinn short shrift. In the nitwit era that we're living through now, it's fashionable, for example, to bad-mouth labor unions and feminists even as workers throughout the land are treated like so much trash and the culture is so riddled with sexism that most people don't even notice it. (There's a restaurant chain called "Hooters," for crying out loud.)

I always wondered why Howard Zinn was considered a radical. (He called himself a radical.) He was an unbelievably decent man who felt obliged to challenge injustice and unfairness wherever he found it. What was so radical about believing that workers should get a fair shake on the job, that corporations have too much power over our lives and much too much influence with the government, that wars are so murderously destructive that alternatives to warfare should be found, that blacks and other racial and ethnic minorities should have the same rights as whites, that the interests of powerful political leaders and corporate elites are not the same as those of ordinary people who are struggling from week to week to make ends meet?

Mr. Zinn was often taken to task for peeling back the rosy veneer of much of American history to reveal sordid realities that had remained hidden for too long. When writing about Andrew Jackson in his most famous book, "A People's History of the United States," published in 1980, Mr. Zinn said:

"If you look through high school textbooks and elementary school textbooks in American history, you will find Jackson the frontiersman, soldier, democrat, man of the people — not Jackson the slaveholder, land speculator, executioner of dissident soldiers, exterminator of Indians."

Radical? Hardly.

Mr. Zinn would protest peacefully for important issues he believed in — against racial segregation, for example, or against the war in Vietnam — and at times he was beaten and arrested for doing so. He was a man of exceptionally strong character who worked hard as a boy growing up in Brooklyn during the Depression. He was a bomber pilot in World War II, and his experience of the unmitigated horror of warfare served as the foundation for his lifelong quest for peaceful solutions to conflict.

He had a wonderful family, and he cherished it. He and his wife, Roslyn, known to all as Roz, were married in 1944 and were inseparable for more than six decades until her death in 2008. She was an activist, too, and Howard's editor. "I never showed my work to anyone except her," he said.

They had two children and five grandchildren.

Mr. Zinn was in Santa Monica this week, resting up after a grueling year of work and travel, when he suffered a heart attack and died on Wednesday. He was a treasure and an inspiration. That he was considered radical says way more about this society than it does about him. (End of Bob Herbert article.)

Next week I'll return to posting information relative to the Charter for Compassion.

31. Serendipity Via e-mail.

When I wrote blog **#7** titled**, "Back to the 'Too Seriously' Dilemma."** I had just learned in March, 2009 that the Charter for Compassion Project was underway.

Now in January, 2010 I receive an e-mail announcing the wording of the completed Charter laser engraved into a handsome, wooden plaque available in English or 10 other languages. The words of the Charter are also available at the following website for free downloading (in a choice of 30 languages) to be transformed into a wall piece for hanging:

http://charterforcompassion.org/share/about/

Here is the final version of the text:

Charter for Compassion

The principle of compassion lies at the heart of all religious, ethical and spiritual traditions, calling us always to treat all others as we wish to be treated ourselves. Compassion impels us to work tirelessly to alleviate the suffering of our fellow creatures, to dethrone ourselves from the centre of our world and put another there, and to honour the inviolable sanctity of every single human being, treating everybody, without exception, with absolute justice, equity and respect.

It is also necessary in both public and private life to refrain consistently and empathically from inflicting pain. To act or speak violently out of spite, chauvinism, or self-interest, to impoverish, exploit or deny basic rights to anybody, and to incite hatred by denigrating others—even our enemies—is a denial of our common humanity. We acknowledge that we have failed to live compassionately and that some have even increased the sum of human misery in the name of religion.

We therefore call upon all men and women ~ to restore compassion to the centre of morality and religion ~ to return to the ancient principle that any interpretation of scripture that breeds violence, hatred or disdain is illegitimate ~ to ensure that youth are given accurate and respectful information about other traditions, religions and cultures ~ to encourage a positive appreciation of cultural and religious diversity ~ to cultivate an informed empathy with the suffering of all human beings—even those regarded as enemies.

We urgently need to make compassion a clear, luminous and dynamic force in our polarized world. Rooted in a principled determination to transcend selfishness, compassion can break down political, dogmatic, ideological and religious boundaries. Born of our deep interdependence, compassion is essential to human relationships and to a fulfilled humanity. It is the path to enlightenment, and indispensible to the creation of a just economy and a peaceful global community.

32. Background Information About the Charter.

The reader can go to the web and find extensive, helpful information concerning the Charter for Compassion Project. A most valuable start can be found at this url:
http://charterforcompassion.org/about
To make it easier for the reader, I shall print into this blog the material found at that url..

ABOUT THE PROJECT

The Charter for Compassion is the result of Karen Armstrong's 2008 TED Prize wish and made possible by the generous support of the Fetzer Institute. It was unveiled to the world on **November 12, 2009**.

Why a Charter for Compassion?

The Charter of Compassion is a cooperative effort to restore not only compassionate thinking but, more importantly, compassionate action to the center of religious, moral and political life. Compassion is the principled determination to put ourselves in the shoes of the other, and lies at the heart of all religious and ethical systems. One of the most urgent tasks of our generation is to build a global community where men and women of all races, nations and ideologies can live together in peace. In our globalized world, everybody has become our neighbor, and the Golden Rule has become an urgent necessity.

The Charter, crafted by people all over the world and drafted by a multi-faith, multi-national council of thinkers and leaders, seeks to change the conversation so that compassion becomes a key word in public and private discourse, making it clear that any ideology that breeds hatred or contempt ~ be it religious or secular ~ has failed the test of our time. It is not simply a statement of principle; it is above all a summons to creative, practical and sustained action to meet the political, moral, religious, social and cultural problems of our time. We invite each of you to adopt the charter as your own, to make a lifelong commitment to live with compassion..

About Karen Armstrong

Karen Armstrong is one of the most provocative, original thinkers on the role of religion in the modern world. Armstrong is a former Roman Catholic nun who left a British convent to pursue a degree in modern literature at Oxford. She has written more than 20 books around the ideas of what Islam, Judaism and Christianity have in common, and around their effect on world events, including the magisterial A History of God and Holy War: The Crusades and Their Impact on Today's World. Her latest book is *The Case for God.* Her meditations on personal faith and religion (she calls herself a freelance monotheist) spark discussion — especially her take on fundamentalism, which she sees in a historical context, as an outgrowth of modern culture.

In February 2008, Karen Armstrong won the TED Prize and wished for help in creating, launching and propagating the Charter for Compassion.

A project of the TED Prize

TED stands for Technology, Entertainment, Design. It is an annual conference which brings together the world's most fascinating thinkers and doers, who are challenged to give the talk of their lives (in 18 minutes). TED.com makes the best talks and performances, the ideas worth spreading, from TED available to the public, for free.

The TED Prize is designed to leverage the TED Community's exceptional array of talent and resources. It is awarded annually to three exceptional individuals who each receive $100,000 and, much more important, the granting of "One Wish to Change the World."

Made possible by the Fetzer Institute

A private operating foundation based in Kalamazoo, Michigan, the Fetzer Institute engages with people and projects around the world to help bring the power of love, forgiveness and compassion to the center individual and community life. The Institute's work rests on a deep conviction that each of us has power to transform the world by strengthening the connection between the inner life of mind and spirit with the outer life of service and action. While the Fetzer Institute is not a religious organization, it honors and learns from a variety of spiritual traditions.

• Learn
• Share
• Act

If the reader will go to the url:

http://charterforcompassion.org/about

and click on each of the three words shown:
Learn, Share, Act – these clicks can open a further wealth of information about the Project.

33. And Here I Digress.

Compassion is the warp and moderation is the weft that will produce fabric from the threads of possibility I am striving to present through this series of blogs. However from time to time I shall present examples of excesses as in, "too religious or too theological."

In the meantime – I digress to report a happening.

As my friends in our Retirement Community have read my previous series as blogs and then as the book, "A Belief System from Beyond the Box," some of them have suggested that we structure a small group to "think beyond the box" on topics which might come to the minds of retired individuals with a lot of time to ponder and discuss. Structuring such a group is not easy. As we started we were reminded of a previous Super Bowl TV ad of Cowboys herding cats.

How many charter members? There were four of us who had expressed hints at possible benefits from some sort of exploratory group. OK, that's a start. We'll expand to other apartment folks and residents from the cottages later. . . if. We'll see how four works out – first.

Where to meet? That was easy – a comfortable lounge on the second floor at Door #3 in the Apartment Building for starters.

When to meet? How long? Not so easy. Finally Friday morning from 9:30 to 10:30 a.m. floated to the top.

How often to meet? Once a week was too often - once a month was too sparse - why, of course, every two weeks.

A name? Since we were choosing to place no limits on our fields of discussion it became obvious that innominate was a term to consider. And thus is borning - The Fortnightly Innominate Society.

"Is borning," it is, because we have no idea whether we will survive the birthing process. We have had one meeting and learned some valuable things – we are diverse – in backgrounds, in beliefs, in expectations, in hopes, in fears. We are diverse in many areas but we are alike in two – we are all retired and of comparable age.

The first meeting is behind us. We chose as our rallying call to revise an anonymous old watchword: "A met need is not a motivator," to a new phrasing – "An unmet need IS a motivator."

Our exclamation at launch, also from the past – (it takes folks of our age group to recognize the opening from Jackie Gleason's early TV Show) – *"And away we go!*

From time to time I shall report, infrequently enough not to bore readers, what the Fortnightly Innominate Society has discussed.

34. Blog #16 Revisited.

Here is a rather long quote from Blog #16 that I shall insert so the reader does not need to go back to look it up:

"As the Universe is expanding and life is evolving, God, as the Atmosphere of Possibilities, is expanding and evolving.

As the previous sentence courses onto my computer's screen, I am reminded of the book, "The Evolution of God," Little, Brown & Company, © 2009, by Robert Wright who traces the stages of human development (hunter-gatherer, agrarian, etc.) and via the religions developed by humans within those stages on into subsequent faith systems (Buddhist, Hindu, Judeo-Christian, Islam, etc.).

Is Wright's book a delineation of the evolution of God or a delineation of the evolution of God religions?

If we stretch our thoughts beyond the physical to a metaphysical Atmosphere of Evolving Possibilities (Rolston) could we then speak in terms of the evolution of God?

To date I have only read a lengthy introduction to Wright's book. When I have completed the book I shall devote a blog or two to my reaction as a layperson.

For now I shall return to the subject at hand.

Does too much passion for any religion, as compared to the

passion of others for their religions, deter the evolution of mutual compassion? History and experience say yes.

Does too much passion for our specific, definitive religion result in our taking our religion too seriously? History and experience say yes."

As I reread this quote I am reminded that conceiving God as the Atmosphere of Possibilities (Rolston) meshes precisely with conceiving God as evolving (Wright).

Through years of exposure to those who, to some, appear to take religion and theology too seriously, I have been amazed that they deem their specific God, who nurtures a Universe of ever changing possibilities, to be infallible and unchanging.

Now -- I've read Robert Wright's book – and a wonderful read it was!

For so many of us old Geezers, who have struggled during most of the 20th Century to overcome the inhibiting, religious conditionings imposed by previous centuries and generations, Wright's book is a breath of fresh air. For our children, who have struggled through much, and our grandchildren, who have struggled through a lesser part, of the 20th Century the book can be a release. For our great grandchildren, the newest generation, the book will be a 21st Century a priori emancipation.

By using recorded facts and discovered artifacts Robert Wright presents the evolving Abrahamic God(s) in believable perspectives, authentic to their "historical times."

Robert Wright introduces us to zero sum and non zero sum human relationships. He traces these relationships from earliest, isolated families of humans, through hunter-gatherer groups, to chieftains, to tribes, to agrarians, to loosely organized clans, to expanding nations. He traces religion from primitive shamans, to polytheism, to monotheism, through Abrahamic Monotheism (Judaism, Christianity, Islam) to Section V of his book – "God Goes Global (Or Doesn't)."

Some readers consider all books pristine objects that are not to be rendered maculate by underlines or notations. I underline material I want to remember and annotate material I want to ponder further or question. I have developed a filing system so that I can refer to such material. All good books have a blank, inside, back cover and really good books always have a blank last leaf. I use these spaces to record the page numbers that I have marked. (Note: At some point in my elementary school career I learned how to place a pencil to paper and without lifting the pencil make five, crossing, straight lines that resulted in a five pointed star. I still delight in making that artistic symbol to mark extra special material. There are many of these stars toward the back of my copy of Wright's book.)

At page 418 - I came to the section on Moral Imagination. Here Wright states:

"The way hatred blocks comprehension is by cramping our "moral imagination," our capacity to put ourselves in the shoes of another person."

On page 430 in Chapter 19 (The Moral Imagination) in Section V - God Goes Global (Or Doesn't) - I bracketed the following quote that directs the matter of "Moral Imagination" to the attention of the reader and in turn to all religions:

"Does the growth of moral imagination conduce to salvation in the sense of individual salvation? Will it save my soul? That is a question for them [religions] to answer as their doctrines continue to evolve. But we can say this much: traditionally, religions that have failed to align individual salvation with social salvation have not, in the end, fared well. And, like it or not the social system to be saved is now a global one. Any religion whose prerequisites for individual salvation don't conduce to the salvation of the whole world is a religion whose time has passed."

From that point to the end of the book, I underlined sentences, bracketed sections and sprinkled my five pointed stars. Of course my conclusive deductions will differ from those of other readers and, no doubt, from those of Author Wright. But to summarize my take on this excellent work here are quotes, and notes, that I consider especially salient.

> • Page 433. "But what the Abrahamic scriptures illustrate, however obscurely, is that there *is* a moral order out there --- and it's imposed on us."
> Page 433-4. "The march of history challenges people to expand their range of sympathy and understanding, to enlarge their moral imaginations, to share the perspective of peoples ever further away.
> Page 434. "What's more, though believing in this moral order doesn't make you believe in God, it may make you, in some sense religious."

(Blogger's note: What I infer from these quotes is that for religions, and their adherents, to be response-able to God, they must be responsible to all of humanity. The words "sympathy and understanding" transpose in my definition to "compassion.")

> • Page 437. "So if the God of the Abrahamic faiths is to keep on doing what he has often managed to do before –- evolve in a way that fosters positive-sum outcomes of non-zero games --- he has some growing to do. His character has to develop in a way that permits, for starters, Muslims, Christians, and Jews to get along as globalization keeps pushing them closer together.
> Page 437-8. "Of course, God's character is a product of the way Muslims, Christians, and Jews think of him. . . .
> For starters, they could think of the different Abrahamic faiths as having been involved, all along, in the same undertaking. And it's true: all three faiths have been struggling to make sense of the world in ultimate terms, in terms of the meaning of it all and the point of it all.

(Blogger's note: Of course, God's character is the product of the way any specific religion (faith, denomination . . .) thinks of him. . . .)

• Page 454-5 "And, anyway, maybe feeling that you're in contact with a personal god *isn't* such a circuitous way to relate to the source of the moral order. I suggested a couple of pages ago that when people feel the presence of a humanlike god, they're drawing on parts of the moral infrastructure built into them by natural selection --- a sense of obligation to other people, guilt over letting people down, gratitude for gifts bestowed, and so on."

(Blogger's note: And here we are response-able to God whose nature is Compassion*, plus we are responsible to our selves who are, in turn, responsible to all of humanity when we demonstrate compassion.)

* I have tried to avoid anthropomorphism by capitalizing the C in God's Compassion.

35. More About Moral Imagination.

As I have been thinking of Robert Wright's term "moral imagination," (standing in the shoes of the other) and how it relates to individual salvation and social salvation, I have come to realize that my concern over morals should be more involved with duration than salvation. How do my morals stand up in the durational relationships of my personal, social, global, universal life rather than what effect will they have on my salvation; whatever, whenever that is? I have to live with my conscience in/for the duration. We certainly will not be responsible for morals when we "have been saved from sin in the *hereafter*," or *whenever.* Hence I won't need a conscience in the hereafter, but it surely is vital to my day to day application of moral imagination and reciprocal altruism (Universal Compassion, The Golden Rule).

Here I will return to Robert Wright's quote on moral imagination and approach it from the perspective of a personal belief system rather than the perspective of a religion:

"Does the growth of moral imagination conduce to salvation in the sense of individual salvation? Will it save my soul? That is a question for them [religions] to answer as their doctrines continue to evolve. But we can say this much: traditionally, religions that have failed to align individual salvation with social salvation have not, in the end, fared well. And, like it or not the social system to be saved is now a global one. Any religion whose prerequisites for individual salvation don't conduce to the salvation of the whole world is a religion whose time has passed."

Does the belief system a specific religion offers, teaches or dictates, include beliefs that preclude the systems of other religions from assisting their adherents in attaining response-able status with God - at least with the God of the religion doing the precluding? (By the way – how is response–able status with God achieved? defined? – I will return to these two essential questions in a later blog, or blogs.)

For now I shall report an article I recently read in Vol. 43. No.1 / February 2010, published in The Layman (A publication of the Presbyterian Lay Committee.) The reader can go to www.layman. org type into SEARCH – "Vol.43,1 / February 2010 Celebrating 45 years in ministry," click on SEARCH, then click on the blue title "Celebrating 45 years of ministry" and there is the article. It may be simpler for readers if I just copy the first four paragraphs of the article into this blog starting here (but I encourage reading the entire article):

"Forty-five years have passed since the formation of the Presbyterian Lay Committee. Most of those years have been tumultuous in the life of the church, as was the year the PLC was established. In 1965 the Presbyterian church was considering adopting a new confession, and many believed the draft was unbiblical and contrary to the foundations of the Reformed faith. The denomination was pushing a new social agenda and they were proposing language in the confession that described God's Word as "nevertheless the words of men ..."

Those few words drew the righteous anger of some Presbyterian elders who believed the new confession would reduce the Bible to everyday literature. They believed this would have a deteriorating effect on the denomination. So a handful of lay leaders met in New York in 1965 and decided to request the denomination's leadership to allow them to publicize their concerns. Their request was denied. They offered to buy space in Presbyterian publications. Again the answer was "no." Not to be denied a voice in the matter, these committed Presbyterians placed full-page ads with their own funds in *The Wall Street Journal, The New York Times, The Washington Post* and other newspapers.

The 1967 General Assembly of the United Presbyterian Church rejected these elders' views and approved the Confession of 1967. The predictions of these elders came true: Biblical illiteracy; an adulterated gospel; a dramatic decline in mission and evangelism; and a massive loss of members.

The founders of PLC were elders who loved Jesus Christ, the Bible and the Presbyterian church. They saw the need for the laity and clergy to be informed of what was happening in the church. They wanted to see a stronger emphasis on the church's mission of spiritual leadership and the importance and authority of the Bible as being the true Word of God, which He has provided for the guidance of all people. They wanted to support and encourage ministers and ruling elders and lay members to be ever mindful that the chief aim and purpose of every Christian is to proclaim that Jesus Christ is Lord and Savior. So in 1968 *The Layman* was born and ever since there has been an abundance of church news to report."

To complete the resource material I shall also copy into this blog the paragraph from the Confession of 1967 as it was actually adopted by the General Assembly of the (then) United Presbyterian Church and as it appears in the Book of Confessions of today's Presbyterian Church USA:

Section 2. The Bible

9.29 The Bible is to be interpreted in the light of its witness to God's work of reconciliation in Christ. The Scriptures, given under the guidance of the Holy Spirit, *are nevertheless the words of men*, conditioned by the language, thought forms, and literary fashions of the places and times at which they were written. They reflect views of life, history, and the cosmos which were then current. The church, therefore, has an obligation to approach the Scriptures with literary and historical understanding. As God has spoken his word in diverse cultural situations, the church is confident that he will continue to speak through the Scriptures in a changing world and in every form of human culture.

The reader can decide whether the phrase, "are nevertheless the words of men," has justified the thousands upon thousands of hours (and dollars) the Presbyterian Lay Committee has expended claiming that: (see following quote from above)

"The predictions of these elders came true: Biblical illiteracy; an adulterated gospel; a dramatic decline in mission and evangelism; and a massive loss of members."

The Presbyterian Lay Committee has chosen to accept and defend the definition from a previous culture that the Bible is "the revealed Word of God." The Committee chooses to base its belief system in this Statement –

"The mission of the Presbyterian Lay Committee is to inform and equip Christians to share the Biblical faith by proclaiming Jesus Christ alone as:
• The Way of salvation.
• The Truth of God's Word.
• The Life of discipleship."

In a previous series of blogs published as a book, "A Belief System from Beyond the Box," page 8, I confronted the following question posed by the Presbyterian Lay Committee: "Can two faiths embrace one future?" (I gather from this question that the Lay Committee is assuming unto itself the status of a faith or a religion?) Here is that page 8 quote:

"Gradually - over its 40 years – [*now 45*] its [*Lay Committee's*] voice has become more strident and its faith system less flexible until it is now a faith within a faith. It is in a more or less adversarial relationship with the mother church and is currently asking the power laden question:

Can Two Faiths Embrace One Future?

The Lay Committee claims impasse with those outside its faith designs and labels anyone who disagrees with its tenets, apostate."

The words of the Bible are human words – formed by humans, utilized by humans, understood by humans. Many Biblical words are beautiful, wholesome, constructive words – befitting the Atmosphere of Possibilities. Unfortunately many Biblical words are ugly, horrific, destructive words – belittling the Atmosphere of Possibilities.

My question: Does the Mission Statement of the Presbyterian Lay Committee and its rigid stand against a confession stating the Scriptures, "are nevertheless the words of men," conduce - or obstruct - moral imagination and universal compassion in the promotion of social salvation?

36. Moral Imagination or Innocent Errancy?

The previous blog #35 closed with this question:

Does the Mission Statement of the Presbyterian Lay Committee and its rigid stand against a confession stating the Scriptures, "are nevertheless the words of men," conduce - or obstruct - moral imagination and universal compassion in the promotion of social salvation?

There are actually two parts to the question. The first part deals with the total Mission Statement of the Lay Committee and the second part deals with a rigid stand against the statement that the Scriptures "are nevertheless the words of men." A rigid stand against defining the scriptures as the words of men needs not obstruct moral imagination in others nor does it conduce others to it. In my opinion it is a typical example of religious persons taking their religion too seriously. **Previous cultures** have stated that God somehow revealed the words of the Judeo-Christian Bible and persons of subsequent faith systems have been conditioned to accept that statement as an "innocent-errancy."

In the Glossary of this and of a previous book, "A Belief System from Beyond the Box," here follows my definition of the coined term, innocent-errancy:

innocent-errancy – a coined term to express the state of believing errant information innocently because it is the best explanation currently available. e.g. The world is flat (1491), the Biblical creation stories, the early concept that the Sun rotated around the Earth.

However - in non-zero-sum exchanges between those of differing religions - if mission (or doctrinal) statements by one party preclude social salvation of the other faith wouldn't this obstruct moral imagination? Proclaiming "Jesus Christ ALONE" as the way to salvation, truth and discipleship does not conduce to inter-faith understanding through moral imagination. Not only does this block social salvation – universal compassion (the Golden Rule) is rendered impossible.

What value does attaining individual salvation extend to those who would deny social salvation to all others. Surely Universal Compassion is one of the component Possibilities contained in the Atmosphere of Possibilities?

37. Another Discovery in the Layman, Vol. 43 No.1.

In the same Volume 43 No.1 of the Layman, wherein I discovered the Presbyterian Lay Committee celebrating its 45 years of existence (see Blog #35), I came upon an article titled – "More than half of PCUSA Presbyterians reject Jesus as sole savior."

This article (byline, The Layman, Posted Tuesday January

12, 2010) may be read online at: http://www.layman.org/News.aspx?article=26639

Here is the entire article as it prints out:

"A recently-released survey by Presbyterian Church (USA)'s Research Services shows that more than half of Presbyterians surveyed reject Jesus Christ as the only way to salvation.

"According to the report entitled "Religious and Demographic Profile of Presbyterians," nearly half of PCUSA pastors (45 percent) and a majority of "specialized clergy" (60 percent) surveyed disagree that "only followers of Jesus Christ can be saved." Approximately 1 in 5 in both categories answered "neutral" or "not sure," making the totals that do not "agree" with the statement as 65 percent for pastors and 78 percent for specialized clergy.

"More than half of "members" and "elders" surveyed answered similarly. Approximately 1 in 3 members (36 percent) and elders (31 percent) either disagree or strongly disagree that "only followers of Jesus can be saved." In both categories, approximately 1 in 5 is "neutral" or "not sure."

"Those who "strongly agree" or "agree" with the statement, according to the survey, are: 39 percent of members; 45 percent of elders; 35 percent of pastors and 22 percent of specialized clergy.

"The report defines "specialized clergy" as ministers serving full-time in a school or seminary, as a hospital or military chaplain, as PCUSA middle governing body staff, in an ecumenical agency or any other job or position. The category also includes part-time and temporary ministries.

"One of several questions posed in the "piety and belief" section, the report also features data on topics such as church activities/involvement, calls/careers and social/demographic characteristics.

"The initial questionnaire, from which the above findings were reported, was sent to more than 5,000 Presbyterians in late 2008, with response rates ranging from 59 to 70 percent from the various groups. The stated average margin of error is around 3 to 5 percent, according to the report, but in some cases can go as high as 7 to 10 percent.

"The first Presbyterian Panel was created in 1973 to inform leaders of the opinions and activities of the denomination's rank and file. The panel is re-established every three years. The current survey group will provide data from the 2009 to 2011 class of panelists. To view the complete report, and others, go to the Research Services Web site."

– – –

Therefore: to see the entire 2008 Report by Presbyterian Church USA Research Services blog readers should go to: http://www.pcusa.org/research/panel/reports/fall08panel.pdf

As one reads the article above it is apparent that it is straight-forward, factual reporting of the "Religious and Demographic Profile of Presbyterians" section of the 2008 Report.

However, the absence of editorial comment by the Layman Staff is not consistent with my experiences as I read their periodical. Opportunities to be critical of the Presbyterian Church USA are rarely passed over in the pressroom of The Layman.

It is but a very short time until the next issue of The Layman, so I shall insert this blog as a "draft" and wait to see what unfolds.

38. An "Aha" Moment!

Vol. 43, No. 2 / March 2010 of the Layman has arrived and on page 6 there is an "Aha" article titled: "Vanishing Christianity – A lesson from the Presbyterians." Commentary by R. Albert Mohler, Jr., President of Southern Baptist Theological Seminary. The article may be found at:

http://www.albertmohler.com/2010/02/11/vanishing-christianity-a-lesson-from-the-presbyterians/

I am not into conspiracy theories. It requires too much effort to understand reality to expend energy on accepting or broadcasting conspiracies. However, I noted that the March, 2010 Layman has gone outside the Presbyterian family to publish a commentary by Dr. Mohler critical of the "Religious and Demographic Profile of Presbyterians" section of the 2008 Report (see blog #37). I wondered if Dr. Mohler had been invited "to offer a lesson TO" Presbyterians, or was this his gracious offer of reciprocal compassion "to save vanishing Christianity" as it is being destroyed by any who do not subscribe to the Presbyterian Layman's Mission Statement that – "*only* followers of Jesus Christ can be saved. "

How much moral imagination does this approach promote/ permit to believers outside the Layman Committee's specific belief system within non-zero-sum ecumenical encounters? How much reciprocal compassion (the Golden Rule) does this display? My blog will not be a critique of Dr. Mohler's article. Who is this layperson to be so presumptuous? My approach will be to explore the validity of the Lay Committee's mission statement: . . . "proclaiming Jesus Christ alone as: The Way of salvation. . ."

I shall ask three questions to assess the validity of the statement.

1. Could the statement be so true that it precludes all other moral imaginations?
2. Could this belief be an innocent errancy?
3. Could the statement be an example of taking a religion too seriously?

Answers:

1. First I would return to Robert Wright's term, "moral imagi-nation" which I introduced in blog # 34, and include the entire paragraph on page 418 from which I quoted the first sentence only.

"The way hatred blocks comprehension is by cramping our moral imagination, our capacity to put ourselves in the shoes of another person. This cramping isn't unnatural. Indeed the tendency of the moral imagination to shrink in the presence of enemies is built into our brains by natural selection. It's part of the machinery that leads us to grant tolerance and understanding to people we see in non-zero-sum terms and deny it to those we consign to the zero-sum category. We're naturally pretty good at putting ourselves in the shoes of close relatives and good friends (people who tend to have non-zero-sum links with us), and naturally bad at putting ourselves in the shoes of rivals and enemies (where zero-sumness is more common). We can't understand these people from the inside."

Who has determined that this "Christ alone" statement must be true for all? Some moral imaginations may be truer than others - but no human imagination can be termed true - just as no human motivation can be termed pure. This is especially accurate when the human thinks beyond/ outside the physical universe into the spiritual Atmosphere of Possibilities.

Just as some religions or groups reduce God to a theistic, anthropomorphic, comprehensible, male deity dictating "God books" to special humans, all of these religions see "their books" as cultural tutorials espousing specific directives for individual salvation within their concept of God. Here I return to Wright's "Evolution of God" thought on individual and social salvation, p. 430:

"But we can say this much: traditionally, religions that have failed to align individual salvation with social salvation have not, in the end, fared well. And, like it or not the social system to be saved is now a global one. Any religion whose prerequisites for individual salvation don't conduce to the salvation of the whole world is a religion whose time has passed."

2. Yes, this is an innocent-errancy. For the human to claim that any human statement expresses a divine revelation is an errancy. Some errancies are more innocent than others. Sometimes the Lay Committee is more innocent than it is at other times. Yes, all of us, including the Lay Committee, err in falling prey to innocent errancies. But what is devastating is that all of us fail to display, or encourage, imagination morality in ourselves and in our religious counterparts as we struggle in non-zero-sum encounters to promote social salvation as well as seek individual salvation.

3. Yes, this is an example of a statement taking religion too seriously. All religions proclaim faith but practice manipulation. I have faith that the teachings of Jesus Christ can be valuable *to me* in this life toward whatever may follow it. When I tell others that Jesus Christ is the *only* way to salvation – I am practicing manipulation.

When universal compassion (the Golden Rule) is manipulated by persons or religions - it is no longer universal (reciprocal) nor is it compassion.

39. By the Way.

The following paragraph appeared in Blog 35.

"Does the belief system a specific religion offers, teaches or dictates, include beliefs that preclude the systems of other religions from assisting their adherents in attaining response-able status with God - at least with the God of the religion doing the precluding? (By the way – how is response–able status with God achieved? defined? – I will return to these two essential questions in a later blog, or blogs.)"

So here I shall speak to my "By the way – how is response–able status with God achieved? - defined?"

In a previous series of blogs that has been published as a book, "A Belief System from Beyond the Box," I condensed my beliefs to this statement –

"I believe that the Incomprehensible God of the Universe is an Atmosphere of Possibilities* within which the human can be a response-able steward to and for the Incomprehensible God – and responsible to and with all of humanity, including self."

*Where did I find the term, " Atmosphere of Possibilities?" Serendipity tapped me on the shoulder in January, 2007 and held out a bright yellow book titled "Genes, Genesis and God, Their Origins in Natural and Human History" by Dr. Holmes Rolston, III.

I quote Rolston from page 367 of that book:

"The divine spirit is the giver of life, pervasively present over the millennia. God is the atmosphere of possibilities, the metaphysical environment, in, with, and under first the natural and later also the cultural environment, luring the Earthen histories upslope."

Now let's return to my belief statement given above and see what I said about it in a November 17, 2008 Blog:

"This is not intended to be a theological statement. It is my *conceptualization* of being response-able to God. It is not a *comprehension* of what we must believe to be saved - **someday**. It is my very own conceptualization for a joyous survival in an atmosphere of possibilities that gets me by - **in these days** - to whatever follows. These statements work for me. That is no proof that they will work for you. Hence you will probably prefer to design your own."

I find God to be incomprehensible. Thus I do not, can not, comprehend a theistic God to whom I pray for a vacant spot in a crowded parking lot or for golden slippers in some hereafter. However, I can conceptualize the possibility that an **open** parking place will develop within the parking lot and I can conceptualize that a **more** joyous life is possible when one is a response-able steward within an Atmosphere of Possibilities.

I cannot determine how others can or should achieve response-able status with God. I cannot define for readers what response-able status with God can or should be for them. Can my peers, some committee, the Council of Nicea in 325 CE, the General Assembly of the PCUSA in 2010 . . . do this for me? No!

Of course, I should be open to all the wisdom and advice available to me from any and all extinct and extant sources, but the unlimited, melodious possibilities within an incomprehensible metaphysical atmosphere do not come to me as rigid, contractual, directives contained in a theistic check-list.

I shall not attempt to tell the reader how to achieve or define a response-able relationship with God. I shall modestly share - *from my side of the equation* - an unvarnished version of what I hope is an authentic, response-able relationship with the Atmosphere of Possibilities that works for me. I make no attempt to offer an appraisal - *for the other side of the equation.*

I shall express my remarks on the subject using a technique employed by Mark Twain. Twain developed an introduction that went something like this:

> "I consider introductions to be unnecessary, but if it is the custom to have them I prefer to do the act myself – so I can depend on getting in all the facts. Tonight, I wish to present a man whose great learning and veneration of the truth are exceeded only by his high moral character and majestic presence. I refer in these vague and general terms to myself. I was born modest, but it wore off – partly - mostly. "

I trust that some of my beliefs are faith and not manipulation. In that light, I also realize that Marcus Borg was accurate when he said in "The Meaning of Jesus" (p. 240):

"One can believe all the right things and remain a jerk, or worse. Saints have been heretical, and people with correct beliefs have been cruel oppressors and brutal persecutors."

40. More About "By the Way."

Time was, when folks greeted me with, "How are you?" I was quick to answer, "Fine, and how are you?"

I have decided to change. Now, depending on who is the asking person, I shall answer, "I'm trying to improve." I'll leave it there. I will not add, "How about you?" They'll be shocked enough – they do not need what might appear to be a put-down response.

In my previous blog #39 I said, concerning my belief statement:

"This is not intended to be a theological statement. It is my *conceptualization* of being response-able to God. It is not a *comprehension* of what we must believe to be saved - **someday**. It is my very own conceptualization for a joyous survival in an atmosphere of possibilities that gets me by - **in these days** - to whatever follows."

Yes, this was my conceptualization but it was not by any stretch my very own conceptualization. In human nature there is indeed – "nothing new under the sun."

I offer the following elementary exercise as an example.

Think of something bizarre. OK – a purple cow. Seems to me I heard a poem once about a purple cow. I go to Wikipedia and feed in "purple cow": "Purple Cow is the name of a well-known poem by Gelett Burgess, first published in the 1895 "Lark.""

I never saw a purple cow
I never hope to see one
But I can tell you anyhow
I'd rather see than be one.

Famously, Burgess became somewhat exasperated with the success of his poem, of which he was constantly reminded. A few years later, he penned a riposte that became almost as well-known as the original. It was titled "Confession: and a Portrait Too, Upon a Background that I Rue" and appeared in The Lark, number 24 (April 1, 1897):

Ah, yes, I wrote the "Purple Cow"—
I'm Sorry, now, I wrote it;
But I can tell you Anyhow
I'll Kill you if you Quote it!.

So I went back to Google and fed in – "I'm trying to improve." I was offered 71,300,000 entries. For "purple cow" I had been offered a mere 795,000 entries.

My point?

My very own conceptualizations are not my *very* own - they come to me in total or as bits and pieces from infinite sources beyond me. This is true of joyous thoughts, not so joyous thoughts and thoughts between. Years ago I heard a poem given as an illustration within a homily. The poem fits the "between" group:

"Once in a saintly passion
I cried with desperate grief,
"O Lord, my heart is black with guile,
Of sinners I am chief."
Then stooped my guardian angel
And whispered from behind,
"Vanity, my little man,
You're nothing of the kind."

I memorized the poem but did not know the author's name. I fed the first line of the poem to Google and learned the name of the poem, "Once in a Saintly Passion," the entire poem, and that James B.V. Thompson was the author. Further I found his tragic biography:

James B.V. Thomson (1834-82) was born in Port Glasgow. He was posted to Ireland in 1851 to work as a schoolmaster in the Army, there he met Charles Bradlaugh, the publisher of the National Reformer which later featured Thomson's work. In 1862, he was dismissed from the Army due to increasing bouts of depression and drinking. He returned to London where he wrote for the National Reformer, whose radical stance matched his own free-thinking and atheistic convictions and latter [sic], when he fell out with Bradlaugh, he wrote for the Secularist, and a house journal from Liverpool called Cope's Tobacco Plant. None of the journalistic and business jobs Thomson undertook in these years lasted very long and he found it difficult to get his creative work published. Thomson died as a result of a final drinking bout in 1882.

I thought how interesting it would have been to know James B.V. Thompson and decide for myself about his, "radical stance [that] matched his own free-thinking and atheistic convictions." His drinking habit was no doubt deleterious and unacceptable, but if the poem reflected his belief system we might have had some fruitful discussions.

Well, I hope readers will not conclude that my modesty has worn off,

"partly or mostly," as I continue to recount what I hope is an authentic, response-able relationship with the Atmosphere of Possibilities – *that seems to work for me.*

41. This Isn't Easy.

It won't be easy to describe how: "response–able status with God is achieved? - defined?"

It is difficult enough to describe how the individual Christian achieves response-able status with God - it is impossible to determine how the diverse Christian Branches can attain response-able status because so many definitions of that status have emerged.

But - as more and more, serious, searching Christians ponder the dilemmas posed by writings such as - "Why Christianity Must Change or Die" (Harper San Francisco, 1998, John Shelby Spong) - achieving or defining response-able status with the Comprehensible God of the Bible Verse becomes more and more remote.

Note: Here I am reminded of a statement from my previous series of blogs that ended in book form, "A Belief System from Beyond the Box." In a November 29, 2007 blog (p. 80 of the book) dealing with the phrase, "Why Christianity Must Change or Die," I offered the following modification:

> The statement, "Christianity must change or die," seems harsh the first time one hears it.
> BUT - The more one observes today's Christian Church mired in contumely, the more validity one perceives in the statement. However, many have come to be more comfortable with the following variant -
> Christianity must morph to survive!
> Note: Survive is the diametrical opposite of die, but morph is not the diametrical opposite of change. Change could be but a degree of morph.
> BUT - How long will metamorphosis require?

Spong's years as a Christian plus years as an official (Bishop) in the hierarchy of the Episcopal Church - and my years as a Christian plus years as a lay elder in the structure of the Presbyterian Church - have brought us to comparable conclusions. Christianity as a religion and the Church as the institutional manifestation of that religion's core beliefs must **morph** those core beliefs and their resultant missions.

How do I defend such "heretical" conclusions?

Universality: Christianity must morph from a dependence upon the comprehensible, theistic God of the Bible Verse to an incomprehensible interdependence with God as the Atmosphere of Possibilities throughout the Universe.

Humanity: Christianity must morph from manipulating individual salvation of its adherents to proclaiming social salvation for all of humanity.

I will offer condensed thinking of separate authors in support of these two concepts:

Universality: No one has presented insights into the universe more astute or prescient than those of Carl Sagan in "The Pale Blue Dot" –

"The Earth is a very small stage in a vast cosmic arena. Think of the river of blood spilled by all those generals and emperors, so that, in glory and triumph, they could become the momentary masters of a fraction of a dot. Think of the endless cruelties visited by the inhabitants of one corner of this pixel on the scarcely distinguishable inhabitants of some other corner, how frequent their misunderstandings, how eager they are to kill one another, how fervent their hatreds, our posturings, our imagined self-importance, the delusion that we have some privileged position in the Universe, are challenged by this point of pale light..."

". . . A religion, old or new, that stressed the magnificence of the Universes revealed by modern science might be able to draw forth reserves of reverence and awe hardly tapped by conventional faiths. Sooner or later such a religion will emerge."

Humanity: If the Golden Rule is true, if universal compassion is valid, the following insight of Robert Wright in "The Evolution of God" is essential to the morphing of any religion.

"But we can say this much: traditionally, religions that have failed to align individual salvation with social salvation have not, in the end, fared well. And, like it or not the social system to be saved is now a global one. Any religion whose prerequisites for individual salvation don't conduce to the salvation of the whole world is a religion whose time has passed."

And now . . . Finality:

I have rambled through Blogs 39, 40 and 41 and finally return to focus on the question: "By the way – how is response–able status with God achieved? - defined?"

Upon returning to the question, I find that the Universe is evolving, human conceptions of God are evolving, religions are evolving . . . in fact prescient humans are predicting such vital departures from tradition as: "drawing forth reserves of reverence and awe hardly tapped by conventional faiths," and "the Evolution of God."

I find that the question has evolved also: **To what conception of God shall I be response-able?**

42. The Throes That Throw Humans.

To what conception of God shall I be response-able?
How can the human be response-able to that which the human cannot comprehend? How has the human dealt with this dilemma?

The ages old response has been to structure a human conception of the Incomprehensible as God and be response-able to that God. The immediate problem arises - how to extend this conception beyond mere imagination. The simple solution – state that the Incomprehensible has the incomprehensible power to communicate definitive information directly to humans as revelations. Some accept this statement as truth, others maintain doubts.

How is this revealed, definitive information saved and utilized? It is preserved through tradition. Thus via **conception, revelation** and **tradition** humans across the ages have been exposed through ever evolving religions to the ever evolving God of the ever evolving Universe. Religions create or accept a conceptual God that those religions **proclaim** to be the true God. The various religions' **manipulations** of God's characteristics or revelations range from micro to macro. Often simple errors in the manual copying or verbal quoting of religious books yield innocent-errancies that morph a religion. Other manipulations are so destructive that a religion must morph away from them to survive, e.g. the absences of moral imagination, compassion, social salvation within a religion,

We are born into cultures and traditions that offer us multiple conceptions of God. Social conditioning or personal choice brings us to a conception of God that we will be response-able or adverse to. Families, society, writers, theologians, committees, institutions, religions enter into our choice of the conception of God we will be response-able or adverse to.

Humans come to believe their conceptions. Too often humanity has come to believe conceptions that contradict universal atmospheres of possibility.

Mark Twain confronted this reality in very straightforward terms:

"There are those who scoff at the school boy, calling him frivolous and shallow. Yet it was the schoolboy who said, "Faith is believing what you know ain't so."

After years of pondering the matter this writer would offer an alternative to the schoolboy's statement:

"Faith is believing what our pinch of spirit, our inner compassion, concludes **is** so."

So –– how accurate is my pinch of spirit, my intrinsic compassion?

43. Staging Spiritual Development.

So –– how accurate is my pinch of spirit, my intrinsic compassion?

At age 12 my grasp of a conception of God was traditionally adequate for my stating in the Beech Grove Presbyterian Church one Sunday Morning in 1936 that I understood and accepted that conception of God as found in my cultural traditions, in the Bible and as confessed by the Constitution of the [then] Presbyterian Church in the United States of America. I trusted that my conceptions at that age were being molded by cultural and traditional conditionings that were vitally interested in my spiritual development and quality of life.

In a previous book, "A Belief System from Beyond the Box," I presented a layperson's chronology of life's stages. The chronology was not intended to be scientific. It was just life as I see it - hopefully as I see it in retrospect from the vantage level of Stage III. Phase 2 in the following chronology.

Stage I. Childhood.
 Phase1. Prior to "Age of Reason." About age 12.
 Phase 2. Up to driving age.

Stage II. Almost Adulthood.

    Phase 1. From driving age to self-sustaining age.

Stage III. Adulthood.

    Phase 1. Inhibited Self-Sustainment.

    Phase 2. Uninhibited Self-Sustainment.

Now, as I prepare to fast forward through my spiritual experiences, I feel the need to present a layperson-friendly staging of spiritual development. My spiritual development has come through infinite sources - seeing flowers bloom. seeing farm animals born, a first viewing of the Grand Canyon from the rim, viewing pictures of the Pale Blue Dot from outer space, being young, being young with our children, being old, being old with our great grandchildren, and through it all struggling with external tradition as it applies to internal fruition.

In this series of blogs I am trying to think and write beyond the box containing the Comprehensible God of the Bible Verse to encounter the Incomprehensible God of the Universe, the Atmosphere of Possibilities. But now as I think back on the spiritual (as a traditional term) portion of my holistic life I realize what a major factor tradition is in our lives and what a huge factor the Bible is in the lives of those within the Christian Tradition.

This is apparent in my Staging of Spiritual Development.

Stage I. Seminal.

Stage II. Early Traditional.

    Phase 1. Pre-Confirmation.

    Phase 2. Post-Confirmation.

Stage III. Traditional.

    Phase 1. Accepting.

    Phase 2. Questioning.

    Phase 3. Morphing.

During the Seminal Stage, the essential energy for an individual's development is supplied by a limited support group. The traditions utilized come through that group.

Self-awareness brings the individual into Stage II termed Early

Traditional. In this stage traditions and conceptions start coming ad infinitum. Many in the Christian Faith believe that there is special significance to being confirmed as part of accepting a precise conception of God. It would appear that for them this act also presumes individual salvation but precludes social salvation for others of our diverse humanity. Other self aware, spiritual folks do not restrict their beliefs through such rituals as confirmation of individual salvation for us and the denial of social salvation for others. This author is not sure if Stage II Phase 1 and Phase 2 are valid distinctions – or traditions irrevocably conditioned into our belief systems.

This author is convinced, however, that Stage III. Phases 1, 2 and 3, is accurate and our spiritual journeys will be fuller and more rewarding if we throw our beings into these throes.

Phase 1. Accepting.

Tradition is not valid until it is accepted.

How it is accepted is vital to my belief system - my acceptance of "Jonah and the Whale" as a myth making a metaphorical point is totally different from my accepting Jonah as a story recounting a true event. Gospel accounts of Christ events can be accepted as supports of Old Testament prophesies or as miraculous, mythical contradictions of physical laws essential to maintaining the Universe and making life possible. It is difficult to accept the possible but it is untenable to cling to the impossible.

Phase 2. Questioning.

Tradition is not valid until it is tested.

Elijah was a prophet in Israel in the 9th century BCE. He raised the dead, brought down fire from the sky and ascended into heaven in a whirlwind accompanied by chariots – although not in one. He was a harbinger of the Messiah. How little noted are harbingers now and how different are the chariots of today!

Christ raised the dead - was himself raised from the dead after three days -ascended. Did these accounts fulfill ancient prophesies or contradict laws essential to the Universe and life?

Does probing and testing ancient mysteries and traditions with today's knowledge constitute heresy?

Phase 3. Morphing.

Tradition is not always valid.

Becoming a tradition does not guarantee that an act or belief rates that description for then or for all time.

Tradition is not irrevocably valid. It is in constant, enigmatic struggle with time and change (morphing). Tradition can render mysteries valid only to have subsequent time and change (morphing) determine that validity to be unsustainable.

It has been my discovery that within my spiritual experiences there is constant tension between tradition and fruition.

44. Time Out for a Letter.

I'll come back to staging my spiritual journey in the next blog.

After I posted the previous Blog 43. I read an excellent article in The Presbyterian Outlook (April 19, 2010) titled "Commissioned Lay Pastors: Second-tier or top-rung leaders." I went beyond reading the article to reviewing the two major references cited. One was an in depth report on 21 Presbyterian Church USA programs producing Commissioned Lay Pastors (CLPs), written by Barbara G. Wheeler (Director of the Center for the Study of Theological Education at Auburn Theological Seminary in New York) a true expert in her field. The other was a 2007 study of CLPs by PC(USA)'s Research Services re: the training of and how presbyteries use CLPs. Both article and research were exemplary in presenting the valuable role less-extensively trained and compensated CLPs could play in the many small congregations unable to afford the ministerial leadership of a full-time, seminary-educated pastor.

I shall not dwell on a comparison of the vocational qualifications of the two levels as leaders in declining-membership, mainline churches. The problem goes so much deeper than leadership preparation and compensation. The problem of declining membership as I see it consists of two major components:

1. The ever more diversified, "Beyond the box of the Comprehensible God of the Bible Verse" belief systems of so many more current adherents and non-adherents of Christianity.
2. The Church's ever more difficult task of teaching ancient, monolithic traditions (via ordained or commissioned teaching elders), and leading adherents with heterogeneous belief systems (via elected ruling elders).

I shall include in this blog a copy of the Letter to the Editor I e-mailed to Presbyterian Outlook on Sunday, May 9. To my surprise the letter appeared in the magazine's website on Monday, May 10 as a response to the article. It will be interesting to follow the reaction of other readers to that letter.

Letter to the Editor,

After I read the article, "Commissioned Lay Pastors," in The Presbyterian Outlook (Vol. 192 No. 8) I read the full remarks of Barbara Wheeler at:
http://www.pcusa.org/vocation/wheelerspeech.pdf
and I reviewed the PCUSA research material at (pcusa.org/clp/).

My response to the article reflects 60+ years as an elder in a small Presbyterian Congregation. I concur with the exemplary insights expressed by both sources above, indicating the critical need for affordable leadership in so many, small congregations during this specific, and continuing, economic era.

However, a question remains, "Will changing the availability and the cost of leadership reverse the losses in membership?"

I shrink from the negative expression, "Christianity must change or it will die." Rather my belief system has struggled and struggled and has finally brought me to a positive alternate, "If Christianity morphs it will survive. "

Tradition is the key.

Tradition is not valid until it is accepted. The Church has indeed accepted traditions – too many of which are difficult for current members and non-members to accept.

Tradition is not valid until it is tested. Does probing and testing ancient mysteries and traditions with today's knowledge constitute a questioning faith -- or unwarranted, automatic heresy?

Tradition is not irrevocably valid. It is in constant, enigmatic struggle -- time and change (morphing) can render mysteries valid only to have subsequent time and change (morphing) determine that validity to be unsustainable.

Edgar K. DeJean, Elder
First Presbyterian Church
Salem, Indiana

45. Discovered – Acres of Diamonds*.

In this blog I intended to return to a further explanation of the oversimplified staging of my spiritual development. In the meantime, while addressing in Blog. 44. an article dealing with the usage of Commissioned Lay Pastors (CLPs) within small congregations of the PCUSA, I coincidentally finished reading the book "Saving Creation; Nature and Faith in the Life of Holmes Rolston III." This is a biography of Dr. Holmes Rolston III by Christopher J. Preston. Readers of this blog series will note my frequent references to the overarching philosophy of Dr. Rolston.

On page 228 in the Epilogue of the Preston biography it was as if a fellow traveler extended a helping hand in the final steps of a struggle forward through tradition to see fruition as a possibility. Here is Preston's summation/analysis of Dr.Rolston's works:

> "Not everyone is convinced that Rolston has articulated the most compelling environmental philosophy. In the last few years, environmental pragmatists have argued that Rolston set the field off in the wrong direction. A core group of urban environmentalists critique what they think is his pro-wilderness bias. Secular Greens don't like the religious elements that linger in the subtext. Consistent with his taciturn nature, Rolston suffers these criticisms silently and

with dignity. He knows that defending ideas, like defending life-forms, is a constant struggle.

The man who has already inscribed the epithet Philosopher Gone Wild onto his gravestone in the family plot at Hebron Presbyterian is a grandfather now. He wonders how much of his grandchildren's lives he will live to see. . ."

Those of traditional bent probably will not interpret the meaning of the phrase Philosopher Gone Wild as I do. I understand the meaning to be that if a theory or philosophy or a belief system deviates sufficiently from what traditionalists proclaim to be Nature -- or the Nature of God -- that believer is judged by the establishment as having Gone Wild.

This blogger is not a professional philosopher, not a theologian. He is a layperson in search of a fulfilling belief system. Perhaps he could consult Dr. Rolston and seek his permission to apply his words, altered slightly, to fit the blogger -- Amateur Philosopher Gone Wild.

* Check: Russell H. Conwell and/or Acres of Diamonds on Google to discover the connection between the phrase, Philosopher Gone Wild and the story about "Acres of Diamonds."
(Next week I promise to get back to my Stages of Spiritual Development.)

46. The Seed Planted.

Now – back to my conceptual outline of my spiritual development:

Stage I. Seminal.
Stage II. Early Traditional.
    Phase 1. Pre-Confirmation.
    Phase 2. Post-Confirmation.

Stage III. Traditional.
  Phase 1. Accepting.
  Phase 2. Questioning.
  Phase 3. Morphing.

Earlier I started to explain the stages and phases of my spiritual journey. As I now reread Blog 43, I realize that I was so fearful of expressing personal example and elaboration that I skipped past an adequate description of how the existential events of one's life transform into the spiritual portion of one's holistic being.

As I recount the events of my life, I have two hang-ups. First, I am fearful that I will project a "too religious" personal portrait and second, I am cautious lest the reader take my words as too directive, "too self-important." I would ask the reader to remember that my words are not wisdom words for their lives – they are survival words for my life. They are words that get me by day to day in this trial and error, exciting existence. It is my hope that the reader accepts and uses them in that manner.

Stage I. Seminal.

An individual does not have control over this stage of his/her spiritual development. Once our family visited the Field Museum of Natural History in Chicago. I was impressed with the elaborate display on genetics, especially one statement - "Having children is hereditary. If your parents didn't, the chances are you won't."

Even though the Seminal phase of our spiritual development occurs before we are capable of expressing self-awareness, we are becoming self-aware. In like fashion the nature of our spiritual awareness is closely aligned with the spiritual awareness of our caretakers during this seminal stage. To mimic the Field Museum quote – "Spiritual awareness is transmissible. If our nurturers didn't have it, chances are we won't."

Although we have minimal control of the Seminal Phase of our Spiritual Development, this does not deny its importance. We can but accept our personal exposure as it has come to us and then edify, or rectify, or nullify our given portion throughout the remaining phases of our lives.

HOWEVER! – in our remaining phases -- within the belief

system we structure to direct our function as response-able to whatever conceptualization of God we acquire – to be truly human, we must maintain responsibility to all humans, **especially those we become privileged to nurture.**

47. Stage II. Early Traditional - Phase 1. Pre-Confirmation.

Stage I. Seminal.
Stage II. Early Traditional.
> **Phase 1. Pre-Confirmation.**
> Phase 2. Post-Confirmation.

Stage III. Traditional.
> Phase 1. Accepting.
> Phase 2. Questioning.
> Phase 3. Morphing.

We can quickly describe the seminal stage of our spiritual development because we do not remember it. Tradition, as conveyed by others, plays the macro role in the seminal stage but we as the subjects within the stage are not yet capable of understanding tradition, even though it is molding our awareness of self and others.

Stage II. Early Traditional - does not refer to traditions generated in early historical times. It refers to all the traditions ingrained into our holistic beings during early development. These traditions come to us through our individual nurturers and through all of our societal and cultural relationships.

Recently I read a newspaper account of a six-year-old boy who was present when his stepfather held his mother's head under water until she drowned. What a horrible event within the transition from the Seminal to the Early Traditional Stage of Spiritual Development for that boy. How fortunate that so few of us transition into the world of awareness bearing the scars of psychic and/or physical trauma. How tragic it is that any child should.

But remember that I am speaking about the nurturers, the culture, the society I knew. Not the ones others may know.

My memories of my transition carry nil numbers of events that even approach being classified as psychic or physical abuse. Oh, one time I threw a hard, green pear at one of my sisters and received a spanking as encouragement not to do it again. I always maintained that if I had hit her there would have been lesser punishment because the miss led to the breaking of an expensive, antique, etched-glass pane in the front door. I learned early that many of life's results are relative.

My spiritual development was not strenuous, cataclysmic nor explosive. As I remember it I just grew up and my spiritual development sort of tagged along.

One time, for some reason, my sisters and I attended worship at the Methodist Church down the road rather than going to the Presbyterian Church. It happened to be a Communion Sunday and a young pastor with young children was supplying the Methodist pulpit. In the staid Services of our particular Presbyterian Church no child took Communion before they were confirmed. Therefore we were amazed when the young pastor's wife gave the elements to her children. Actually my older sisters and the Methodists were amazed. I thought it was pretty neat myself.

But I'm not done. After church when the pastor's family was preparing to leave, his wife gave their little girls some of the left over bread. Being seven or eight at the time, as I have remembered the event, I was the only local in the Methodist Church that Sunday who was not in shock over the event.

I was not into hierarchy at the time so I do not remember how high up the hierarchy of the Methodist District the matter went.

Often, I have wondered if my liberal bent had some of its beginnings within the brouhaha over that event.

I am not downplaying the importance of these early developmental years before the so-called Age of Reason or Confirmation Age. I can only state that during those years I felt no weight of spiritual development pressing down upon my holistic being. In fact I had no concept of what my holistic being was.

48. Stage II. Phase 2. Post-Confirmation.

Stage I. Seminal.
Stage II. Early Traditional.
Phase 1. Pre-Confirmation.
Phase 2. Post-Confirmation.
Stage III. Traditional.
Phase 1. Accepting.
Phase 2. Questioning.
Phase 3. Morphing.

As I reviewed the previous two blogs, in preparation for this one, it came to me that I should be careful not to give the appearance of rating the stages and phases as to significance.

It seems to me our holistic being is a lifelong melodious composition, with each note exposed, not a rigid structure where weak bricks can be hidden.

If we approached people on the street and asked, "Are you saved?" most would understand the question. Ubiquitous traditions have created this reaction.

If we asked, "Have you gone through Confirmation?" we might receive several blank looks. Deficits within tradition permit this vacuum within many folks.

Not only do religions have their traditions, they have their jargons that explain those traditions.

The fact that I have divided the Early Traditional Stage into Pre-Confirmation and Post-Confirmation Phases should not indicate a disproportionate importance of the two phases. This, in my mind, would be a perfect example of how religions abuse traditions.

Name a tradition, a sacrament, a doctrine, a tenet, a myth, a metaphor, an anecdote, etc. - compare how the process of change has altered it from one religion or culture to another -- then seek an answer to this question –

Do we humans use tradition accurately or do we confuse and abuse traditions?

My nurturing family and community did not hold that Confirmation or Joining Church, or Accepting Christ was a Born Again event. It was an important existential psychological-mental event within myriad, ongoing events that somehow transform into the metaphysical spiritual component of my holistic being. My nurturers did not confuse nor abuse tradition. They offered me the tradition of developing within that atmosphere of possibilities in which my unique self could develop.

My grandmother ran a country store where she had a very comfortable chair available when a lack of customers took her off duty. A well-worn Bible was at hand but she often admitted that she wondered how parts of it made the grade. The morning mail brought the daily newspaper. She also wondered how much of its contents could be deemed newsworthy.

I remember family discussions of politics. My maternal grandmother was a Republican, my mother and father Democrats. There were no discussions of Creationism, or Intelligent Design or whatever the process was called as I was growing up. My father was a schoolteacher, firmly in Darwin's camp, and the rest of the family was also in residence there.

In high school I dated an attractive girl from a very fundamental church. We had a great relationship and it made my last couple of years of high school a pleasant era of my life. Religion was not high on our list of conversations.

When I went away to college she discovered a young man of her family's religious persuasion who was the perfect match – so all's well that ends well.

Later at college I met a beautiful Episcopalian girl. I hadn't known any Episcopalians in my community but their belief system seemed to track with Presbyterianism so three years later (67 years ago) we were married. The only reason I am still a Presbyterian – there was no Episcopal church in the town where we settled after WWII.

As I stated in Blog 47. –

I learned early that many of life's results are relative.

49. Stage III. Traditional. Phase 1. Accepting.

Stage I. Seminal.
Stage II. Early Traditional.
    Phase 1. Pre-Confirmation.
    Phase 2. Post-Confirmation.
Stage III. Traditional.
    Phase 1. Accepting.
    Phase 2. Questioning.
    Phase 3. Morphing.

Within my schema of spiritual development (Stage II. Early Traditional) tradition is a directive force defining the emerging spirituality. Within this schema (Stage III. Traditional) tradition is a passive force maintaining that spirituality. Thus Early Traditional differs from Traditional in application rather than chronology.

I realize that the impact of tradition shifts back and forth between defining and maintaining but I am striving to demonstrate the phases that we go through as we react to tradition.

If tradition is to become a defining force within our spiritual development, it must be accepted - hence Stage III, Phase 1. Even though we may question the tradition it is imperative that we accept it to some degree if we are to receive any of the directive force or benefits it may contain.

Tradition can be fact or fiction; accurate statement or conundrum. Nowhere is tradition more confusing than in the realm of religion. Whether or not historical George Washington threw a dollar coin across a body of water named the Delaware River is far less significant as tradition than whether historical Jesus walked across a body of water named the Sea of Galilee. Either tradition could represent fact or fiction; accurate statement or conundrum.

The acceptance of tradition is relative. Christianity pays little heed to acceptance or non-acceptance of George's toss, but to some Christians I am apostate if I do not accept Jesus' watery walk as a literal, historical event worthy of valid, religious tradition. In our younger years we must choose carefully the traditions we accept, even as we are not capable of accurate choices. Thus it falls upon our nurturers to be responsible in the traditions they present as authentic.

But most important of all it falls to religions as nurturing institutions of all their adherents to promulgate communal belief systems based on valid, authentic traditions.

50. Stage III. Traditional. Phase 2. Questioning.

Stage I. Seminal.
Stage II. Early Traditional.
    Phase 1. Pre-Confirmation.
    Phase 2. Post-Confirmation.
Stage III. Traditional.
    Phase 1. Accepting.
    Phase 2. Questioning.
    Phase 3. Morphing.

The acceptance of beliefs and traditions within a religious context gradually evolves our faith system, that system through which we are response-able to our conception of God and responsible to our awareness of humanity. This evolution is life long and **to be of value** must be under continuing review and evaluation. Unfortunately, this principle is counter to the actual practices of religions.

History assures that all religions share the innocent-errancy of declaring infallibility as they proclaim comprehension of the incomprehensible. Religions do not react well to being questioned. Religions are universal in the assumption that questioning their beliefs and traditions will diminish the loyalty of (or the religion's control over?) adherents. Yes, questioning the beliefs and traditions of a given religion is a questioning of the Very God who shared those beliefs and traditions with that religion. And, of course, this Very God is the only God there is.

Is it possible that this observation prompts Robert Wright to make the following statement in The Evolution of God (page 430)?

". . . Like it or not, the social system to be saved is now a global one. Any religion whose prerequisites for individual salvation don't conduce to the salvation of the whole world is a religion whose time has passed."

The number of beliefs and traditions available for human acceptance is limitless. This means that the number of beliefs and traditions we can question is limitless. I am sure there are readers who wonder why I picked on George Washington and the dollar toss and Jesus and the water walk. There was no profound reason. They just "popped" into my flow of thought. I am sure that there are readers who would prefer that I forget George and the dollar as an insignificant "father of the country tale." I am sure that some of these same readers can't understand how one could question as illustrative myth rather than accept as literal truth a story of Jesus walking on water -- **since it appears as a part of Biblical tradition**.

In my later years I have had to make the ultimate decision that the thinking human faces. If I am to be passionately response-able to a functional concept of God and compassionately responsible to humanity, how do I structure my faith from valid beliefs and traditions? First - it has to be **my** faith. It cannot be the "Faith of Our Fathers living still." Second - it does not need to be a faith in a Magical God authenticated by impossible events. The Incomprehensible God does not need to countermand the laws that render the universe stable (e.g. the density of water and gravitational forces).

The Incomprehensible God of the Universe(s) needs to be, **and to offer,** an "Atmosphere of Possibility that lures humankind upslope." (Rolston)

As a human I need to question the traditions and beliefs on which I base my faith - do they lure me upslope to be response-able to a sustainable concept of God and do they lure me up the responsible slope of reciprocal altruism and compassion with my fellow humans?

For my definition of faith I revert to the end of Blog 42 and quote:

"Faith is believing what our pinch of spirit, our inner compassion, concludes is so."

And I repeat the question that followed –

"So –– how accurate is my pinch of spirit, my intrinsic compassion?"

51. Stage III. Traditional. Phase 3. Morphing.

Stage I. Seminal.
Stage II. Early Traditional.
    Phase 1. Pre-Confirmation.
    Phase 2. Post-Confirmation.
Stage III. Traditional.
    Phase 1. Accepting.
    Phase 2. Questioning.
    Phase 3. Morphing.

As I question the existing beliefs and traditions within my faith system, I test them against new knowledge and facts.

The first test is – do changed beliefs and traditions render my pinch of spirit more response-able to my conceptualization of God, the Atmosphere of Possibilities?

The second test is – do changed beliefs and traditions render my intrinsic compassion more responsible to humanity, the essence of reality.

"So –– how accurate are my pinch of spirit, my intrinsic compassion?" When it comes to questioning and morphing my belief system how well does my holistic being come off in this swap under the guidance of my spiritual, catalytic converter?

An interesting thought has occurred to me. It is accepted fact (scientific not urban myth) that our physical being undergoes a total change of cells (and atoms!) over varying time frames for various tissues. A simple rule is stated as seven years but this is not accurate for all tissues and certainly not for all ages. I would suggest that the reader will find it most interesting to Google the term:

"Cellular Longevity and Entire Body Replacement"

Or go directly to the following website:

http://answers.google.com/answers/threadview/id/552383.html

How thrilling to just turn our minds loose on that good old unstable/stable word:

EVOLUTION

The Universe is evolving. Planet Earth is evolving. Physical life is evolving. Every so often we get new bodies. Our holistic beings (open to ever evolving Atmospheres of Possibility) transform ever-changing existential events into spiritual developments, pinches of spirit plus intrinsic compassions, all of which are constantly evolving.

It is my hope that this blog summarizes the periodic questioning and morphing of my personal belief system within my course of spiritual development.

In the next blog I shall tackle the indescribably more difficult morph – the morphing of Communal Christianity - **if it is to survive.**

52. Can Christianity Morph?

It is late morning but still quite dark and filled with angry thunder and flashing bolts. If I believed in a conceptualized, theistic, directive god I would assume that he has looked over my shoulder and is trying to dissuade me from penning a blog under the title above. The morning reminds me of a story my friend Pastor Bill sent me recently:

The funeral party was under the tent in the cemetery and the preacher had just completed the words of condolence and promise to the husband, family and friends of the deceased. Suddenly there was a flashing bolt of light then an earth-shaking roar of thunder - followed by a long, low, seemingly endless growl. The husband turned to the preacher and said calmly, "Well, Pastor, she's there."

I do not mean to make light of human death or the profound travail of morphing our Christian faith; but the former is inexorable and the latter is inevitable. There is no need to explain the former to any of our peers. There is no way to explain the latter to too many of our peers.

There are multitudinous persons in all the many religions of the world who have grasped, through their pinches of spirit and intrinsic compassions, ways to be response-able to God and responsible to humanity. These recognitions give me the temerity to deny that I am anti religion. However, as I observe the general patterns of religious practice on our pale blue dot, I feel compelled to repeat Robert Wright's statement in "The Evolution of God:"

> ". . . Like it or not, the social system to be saved is now a global one. Any religion whose prerequisites for individual salvation don't conduce to the salvation of the whole world is a religion whose time has passed."

I shall not speak of any religion other than my own Christian Faith. I am convinced that it would be a long term disaster if Christianity's "time has passed" – e.g. if Christianity dies before it can morph beyond a prerequisite for "individual salvation" to actually **practicing** salvation for the whole of humanity instead of merely **proclaiming** it for a select few.

Just as I discerned early that the events of life are relative (e.g. the green pear that broke the antique, glass pane) I have come to discern that humans' wishes for the morphing of their religions are relative – relative to times and conditions. As our physical cells and atoms are constantly being exchanged, the existential events contributing to our spiritual developments are altered, our pinches of spirit and intrinsic compassions evolve and our belief systems are morphed.

Yes, the morphing of our bodies, our pinches of spirit, our intrinsic compassions, our belief systems - is tedious and complicated - but what is more vital to the evolution of our holistic beings? Yes, but isn't morphing Christianity also vital to its continuing survival as a religion - response-able to God and responsible to all humanity of the pale blue dot?

"Can Christianity Morph?"

Of course it can!

It's been doing it ever since it was a twinkle in the Atmosphere of Possibilities!

53. Of Course It Can

When I was growing up the grandmother of one of my friends had some framed words in a prominent spot in her kitchen. There were three very short linesof type in large script readable from most of the room:

The Bible says it,
I believe it,
That settles it.

I have puzzled whether to insert my memories of that household sign into a blog dealing with the "too religious" or this blog dealing with the morphing of the Christian Faith. As I remember these good folks they didn't really fit my current category of "too religious." Add to that the fact that I remember having a boyhood conversation with my grandmother about the sign. I asked her what the sign meant. She said she had seen the sign, that it had been put up by my friend's, grandmother's, deceased mother who was very set in her ways and my grandmother couldn't figure out "why she (the current owner) doesn't take it down since she's not a bit like her mother was." As I remember my Grandmother's conclusion, it was, "Over the years that family and the church they go to have changed their religion <*a long pause*> for the better."

Over the years I have seen instance after instance of persons, families, churches, even religions morphing, as my grandmother put it -- "for the better."

When it comes to reading the Bible literally the Christian Faith is morphing – sometimes very slowly – but still morphing. When Jesus is quoted as saying in the Bible (RSV, John 14-6) "I am the way, and the truth, and the life; no one comes to the Father, but by me," and a reliable poll of Presbyterian Church USA members and clergy concludes that approximately 50% do not believe that Christianity is the ONLY way to salvation – this has to indicate morphing – at least in the PCUSA.

Can Christianity morph?

Of course it can!

It already has.

Christianity morphed to fit the Jewish temple worship.

Christianity morphed to fit the Jewish scriptures.

Christianity morphed to fit Jewish traditions and holy days.

Christianity morphed to fit the Greek and Roman cultures.

Christianity morphed to fit differing creeds.

Christianity morphed to fit one God into a Trinity.

Christianity morphed to fit reformed governance.

. . . And the "morphed to fit" existential changes go on . . .

One of our delightful vacations was a two week pilgrimage to Ireland with our daughter Yvonne and husband Tom, their daughters Maggie and Annie, Tom's parents William and Mary Lou McShane. A small bus, full of the ecumenical, driven by our congenial-guide Tony, an Irish Catholic, visited numerous cousins of William McShane.

Faith and Begorrah - don't get me started on the wonderful tales of that trip.

In an Irish Cemetery, Tony supplied us with a wonderful bit of evidence dealing with the morphing of Christianity. When we were in the area where St. Patrick converted the Druids from worship of the Sun to worship of the Son, Tony explained the origin of the Celtic Cross. In order to combine the symbol of the Christian Cross with the circle of the Moon worshippers St. Patrick simply imposed the cross on the circle.

I find that Wikipedia supports Tony's explanation:

"There is a legend of how St. Patrick when preaching to some soon-to-be converted heathens was shown a sacred standing stone that was marked with a circle that was symbolic of the moon goddess. Patrick made the mark of a Latin cross through the circle and blessed the stone making the first Celtic Cross. This legend implies that the Saint was willing to make ideas and practices that were formerly Druid into Christian ideas and practices. This is consistent with the belief that he converted and ordained many Druids to lives as Christian priests."

I remember Tony's observation – "Wonder where we Christians got the idea that we're supposed to think absolutely alike about so many little things?"

54. So Many Little Things.

Neither Tony nor I are so naïve as to think that Christian creeds, doctrines, scriptures, symbols, tenets and traditions are "so many little things." But our wonder is, if we all have the capability of diversity, why does our religion insist on unanimity within our belief systems?

I also have the sly wonder – did St. Patrick "Seize the day?"

Would a Christian-Druid Committee, meeting as the Council of Ireland, have ever come up with such a simple solution as a Celtic Cross?

Humans say – "All humans are created equal."

Where is the conclusion – "All humans are equally response-able to God."

Religions say as self-justification - "Our system of belief was dictated to us by God."

But, actually, humans conceptualize separate religions – ours' more and others' less -- response-able to God.

Any religion will fail eventually unless it seeks social salvation by celebrating diversity instead of seeking individual salvation by demanding unanimity. (Robert Wright p. 430, "The Evolution of God" paraphrased)

Two human deficits:

Humans fail to comprehend that all humans are equally human – hence they conceptualize separate religions. All religions fail to comprehend that the God religions cannot comprehend is Universal – hence they conceptualize separate gods.

Christianity, per its Bible and Traditions, conditions us, as adherents, to claim unanimity with God through Christ. This fulfills Christianity's equation of being response-able to God. It also fulfills Christianity's claim to be responsible to all of humanity - but **ONLY IF** humanity believes in Christianity's Triune God. The "only if" takes celebrating diversity out of the equation of being responsible to all of humanity through seeking social salvation.

So here we are again – "Christianity must change or die."

Or the softer version – "Christianity must morph to survive."

I'll ponder a week.

55. I've Pondered.

I have indeed pondered for a week, and I have survived. What is the basis of that survival? How to explain it?

Have I been under the aegis, not, mind you, the theistic directives, of the Incomprehensible God, the Atmosphere of Possibilities, luring me upslope because there are still possibilities in me? Or is the Comprehensible God of the Bible Verse, who turned Lot's wife into a pillar of salt, too busy with other individuals at the moment?

I shall turn to an American humorist for an answer. Mark Twain explained his deficiency of orthodoxy this way: "My advances in Presbyterianism were not at a rate sufficient for my mother, but apparently adequate to restrain the lightning which she assured me was constantly aimed my direction."

In times past, when I was rebuked as apostate by some of the orthodox, I would take exception and object to the term. As I have pondered more I have concluded that I should thank them for the redefinition.

But I digress.

It is my conclusion - this blog series has now established that my personal belief system has morphed from the Comprehensible God of the Bible Verse to the Incomprehensible God of the Universe, the Atmosphere of Possibilities. My immediate society seems to accept this morphed me as a healthy, holistic being.

Nor has Mark Twain's, mother's, predicted lightning struck me down.

But now I am at the point of presenting the case that Christianity must morph if it is to survive. I arrive at this conclusion from the universal existential and not from personal hallucinations or imaginations.

I go back to Blog 53. to find the question –

"Can Christianity morph?

Of course it can!

It already has.

Christianity morphed to fit the Jewish temple worship.

Christianity morphed to fit the Jewish scriptures.

Christianity morphed to fit Jewish traditions and holy days.

Christianity morphed to fit the Greek and Roman cultures.

Christianity morphed to fit differing creeds.

Christianity morphed to fit one God into a Trinity.

Christianity morphed to fit reformed governance.

And the "morphed to fit" existential goes on . . ."

I find more and more "wondering" people. Not people whom I grab by the lapels and ask, "Are you wondering?" No! I find more and more people who are wondering on their own, "How does religion morph from promising individual salvation to celebrating diversity within universal salvation?"

I am blessed to live in a community with folks who realize that their days are short and they want those days to be lived in comfortable bodies with stress- free minds. They have come to realize that life is more about relating than competing or dominating. (Oh, a few in the Bridge-O-Rama Group haven't gotten the message, but they serve the purpose of – "those whom we need to understand.")

There are exceptions but, by and large, these peers have arrived at a deeper understanding and appreciation of social salvation rather than holding a "too religious" fetish for individual salvation. They celebrate diversity all week and only think briefly of unanimity of belief when they go out into the world on Sabbath occasions.

Extensive literature, past, present and future, has and will explain how humans can and do morph their individual belief systems to strive for holistic lives in the Ever-Changing Atmosphere of Possibilities. In an earlier series of blogs that became the book, "A Belief System from Beyond the Box," I summarized these beliefs in this statement:

> "I believe that the Incomprehensible God of the Universe is an Atmosphere of Possibilities within which the human can be a response-able steward to and for the Incomprehensible God – and responsible to and with all of humanity, including self."

Here I shall try to summarize the morphing process that can bring individual humans to this belief:

> To be response-able to Incomprehensible God I must contemplate God's gift of Grace and translate it into the human compassion that renders me responsible to seek social salvation for all of humanity including myself.

Extensive sources, past, present and future, have and will explain how specific religions can and do morph their belief systems to strive for holistic lives of adherents in the Ever-Changing Atmosphere of Possibilities. Here I shall try to summarize the morphing process that can produce religions capable of assisting adherents:

> To be response-able to Incomprehensible God, religions must contemplate God's gift of Grace and assist humans in translating it into compassion that renders them responsible to seek social salvation for all of humanity.

So, now -- I hope that I have pondered morphing into a few helpful words rather than into overwhelming lists of do's and don'ts.

56. So, now –

The house is gone – the one where I first saw the kitchen-wall sign that I quoted in Blog 53.

The Bible says it,
I believe it,
That settles it.

Change happens. That's why I am suggesting a morphed sign with these words replacing the ones I had seen on that kitchen wall of my youth.

This is Possible.
We believe it.
Let's do it!

This is Possible.
It is possible to worship God as the Incomprehensible God of the Universe, the Atmosphere of Possibilities, luring the human upslope. After all Yahweh went through several conversions before "He" was conceptualized as the God of Abraham, and then over centuries came to be the Comprehensible God of the Bible Verse. Even though the human cannot comprehend the limitless Atmosphere of Possibilities we surely can comprehend that God is infinitely more complex than a limited anthropomorphic, "He" version of the human.

We believe it.
We believe that Grace (God as Love) abounds in the Atmosphere

of Possibilities and is available to all humans for transformation to a compassion that renders social salvation immanent over individual salvation.

Let's do it!
Can Christianity morph?

57. Can Christianity Morph?

Is the answer, "We can start," from within the Atmosphere of Possibilities?

"A man has made at least a start on discovering the meaning of human life when he plants shade trees under which he knows full well he will never sit."

Dr. David Elton Trueblood

A paragraph follows - from the WayNet Biography at:
http://www.waynet.org/people/biography/trueblood.htm
of D. Elton Trueblood - December 12, 1900 to December 20, 1994.

"Elton Trueblood's English Quaker ancestors settled on the coast of North Carolina in 1682 at the site of the present town of Elizabeth City. In 1815 a large Quaker group, including the Trueblood's, emigrated to Washington County, Indiana, to become a vital part of a new Friends community. In 1869 Elton Trueblood's grandfather and other members of the family moved to Warren County, Iowa, where he was born on a small farm near Indianola on December 12, 1900, the son of Samuel and Effie Trueblood."

The Quaker Community left its imprimatur on Washington County through the establishment of the Salem Peace Society in 1818 and through churches and a school structured in the next few decades. Elton Trueblood spent miniscule portions of his life in Washington County, Indiana attending reunions of his family heritage and sharing his wisdom through addresses at these events. Many of us who spent most of our lives in Washington County came to meet Elton Trueblood in these brief moments as well as through his writings.

In this blog I would introduce the reality that Christianity will not morph within a foreseeable time frame. But this does not excuse us from attempting the two vital imperatives within the totality of life – being response-able to God and being responsible to all humanity (including self).

We do make "at least a start on discovering the meaning of human life" when we grasp the synergistic concepts that we are response-able to Incomprehensible God and responsible to comprehensible humanity.

58 . Again - Can Christianity Morph?

What if the answer is – "No?"

Seems to me the answer can be, "No," from two perspectives:

The first "No" would assure us that Christianity is the perfect religion, somehow delivered to humanity as infallible. No morphing necessary, or even possible.

A contravening, second "No" would warn us that we have not examined Christianity objectively enough to know whether it should or could be morphed.

Context is everything. The following quote from Dr. Trueblood would appear to support the first perspective:

"The world is equally shocked at hearing Christianity criticized and seeing it practiced."

Conversely the following Trueblood quote, perhaps taken out of context (I can't find the original text) could appear to support the second perspective:

"The unexamined faith is not worth having."

I do not pretend to interpret Dr. Trueblood's intent within this quote. Is it intended to classify those who do, or those who do not, examine their faiths; or is it encouragement to study what we believe?

Whatever? On face value alone, the unexamined faith is not worth having.

No matter how one believes the Christian Belief System was designed and delivered, by God or by humankind, if examined adequately, the System includes enough contradictions that it cannot be ruled infallible and it excludes enough humans that it cannot be judged compassionate.

Either way morphing is essential.

59. The First "No" Perspective Reviewed.

Continued from Blog 58.

"What if the answer is – "No?"

Seems to me the answer can be, "No" from two perspectives:

The first "No" would assure us that Christianity is the perfect religion, somehow delivered to humanity as infallible. No morphing necessary, or even possible."

What I share next is an acquired doubt expressed in a questioning manner.

As a child I knew – "God is Great, God is Good – and we thank him for our food." I was conditioned to believe that the Comprehensible God of the Bible Verse doesn't change. It followed naturally that God's Church's belief system does not need to change either.

Later, during the young adult development of my belief system, I was exposed to the persuasion that Christianity is not actually a religion. A belief system so transcendentally designed and endowed as Christianity, has to be the only, unique, sacred connection to the Transcendent. This was not only a huge problem to one searching for a belief system it was a huge problem for seminal Christianity searching for adherents.

The human has a built in propensity for three dimensional thought: length, width, height; land, sea, air; good, better, best; Father, Son, Holy Spirit. Even when a tripartite pattern is not obvious the human mind structures one. God is Infallible. Christianity is Infallible.

Christianity is the only Infallible connection between the fallible human and Infallible God.

As the Christian belief system gradually evolved carrying its factional, contentious explanations and doctrines it became more and more effective for some adherents to change the system from following the teachings of Jesus to sharing in the very being of Christ as a transcendental bridge from fallible human to Infallible God. Thus the Council of Nicea and the years following enhanced the Trinity as the ultimate solution and Christianity became an infallible, transcendental bond instead of a religion.

Hence the question becomes - **Can an infallible, transcendental bond be morphed?**

An Addendum:

Some experiential events of life are simply too human and too illustrative to remain untold, even though the telling may tax reverence in some staid minds. One of Elinor's and my best friends for over 50 years together in the same church was very conservative when our friendship started. We were equally liberal. There was no hesitancy on either side to state beliefs. Nor could any younger couple have respected a true matron of the church more than we respected her.

The church even seemed to profit through the counterbalancing support from both sides of this relationship. As the years went by both sides of a remarkable friendship grew toward moderation in all things, per the age-old Presbyterian standard. At one church supper Helen appeared in a new sweatshirt – a gift from an unknown admirer.

It was imprinted:

I am not ~~INFALLABLE~~
INFALLIBLE
I Am Just Always Right!

This sweatshirt got lots of wear and Helen used the slogan to her advantage on many opportune occasions. She was survived by a son and a daughter possessing her streak of exemplary human nature and - "the rest of the story is" -

Helen was buried in this, her most prized sweatshirt.

60. Can An Infallible, Transcendental Bond Be Morphed?

How did I arrive at the term – " infallible, transcendental bond?"

Human tripartite logic over the past two millennia has presented the following (see Blog 59):

> "God is Infallible. Christianity is Infallible. Christianity is the only Infallible connection between the fallible human and Infallible God."

Let's explore this logic step by step.

God is Infallible.

I cannot imagine, and I certainly cannot discern, anything more impossible than for the human to define or comprehend the nature of God. In contrast I can think of no single task that humans spend more time on than defining and comprehending God. One of the great stress-eliminating moments of release in my life was the one in which I concluded that God is the Indefinable, Incomprehensible God of the Universe, the Atmosphere of Possibilities, as contrasted with the humanly definable, comprehensible God of the Bible Verse, the climate of infallibility. With that release came my recognition that whether God is infallible or not is God's business and I should concentrate on correcting my fallibility as my business.

How I learned about God's business:

One time I was privileged to facilitate a course studying The Reformed Tradition within a presbytery program developing Commissioned Lay Preachers (term used then) in the Presbyterian Church USA. One of the class members, Sally, was from a background based in the tradition of "That old time religion." When Sally found herself in a theological corner where her old time religion was not sufficient to provide escape, she had a standard statement – "Well, that's God's business, and what God does is God's business."

It is difficult to refute that what God does is God's business. Another wisdom saying from that old time religion is, "God alone, knows."

Back to the question, "Is God infallible?" I prefer the irrefutable triplet;

> "God alone knows, that's God's business, and
> what God does is God's business."

Christianity is infallible.

This was an early problem within Christendom, but a few weeks of intensive theological bickering at the Council of Nicea plus a couple of centuries of extensive human tweaking throughout Christendom and the triune loop was complete. Thus Christianity leapfrogged the status of being a religion to become the -- **only, Infallible connection between the fallible human and Infallible God – The Infallible Transcendental Bond.**

61. The Second "No" Perspective Reviewed.

To quote from Blog 58. "Can Christianity Morph?"

> "What if the answer is – "No?"
> Seems to me the answer can be, "No," from two perspectives:
> The first "No" would assure us that Christianity is the perfect religion, somehow delivered to humanity as infallible. No morphing necessary, or even possible.
> A contravening, second "No" would warn us that we have not examined Christianity objectively enough to know whether it should or could be morphed."

It becomes obvious that the two "No" answers are synergistically reinforcing.

The first No is supported by the direct transcendental perspective that the Infallible God has delivered a perfect belief system to imperfect humans and thus the system is impervious to change or morphing.

The second No is supported by the conditioned human perspective that the Christian Faith could not have derived from the incidental minds of humans and hence there is no purpose to studying it objectively with the goal of morphing it.

To ease the reader's searching of previous blogs, I shall insert here the last several paragraphs and conclusions of Blog 55:

"Extensive sources, past, present and future, have and will explain how humans can and do morph their individual belief systems to strive for holistic lives in the Ever-Changing Atmosphere of Possibilities. In an earlier series of blogs that became the book, "A Belief System from Beyond the Box," I summarized these beliefs in this statement:

> "I believe that the Incomprehensible God of the Universe is an Atmosphere of Possibilities within which the human can be a response-able steward to and for the Incomprehensible God – and responsible to and with all of humanity, including self."

Here I shall try to summarize a morphing process that could bring individual humans to this belief:

> To be response-able to Incomprehensible God I must contemplate God's gift of Grace and translate it into the human compassion that renders me responsible to seek social salvation for all of humanity including myself.

Extensive sources, past, present and future, have and will explain how specific religions can and do morph their belief systems to strive for holistic lives of adherents in the Ever-Changing Atmosphere of Possibilities. Here I shall try to summarize the morphing process that can produce religions capable of assisting adherents:

> To be response-able to Incomprehensible God religions must contemplate God's gift of Grace and assist humans in

translating it into compassion that renders them responsible to seek social salvation for all of humanity.

So, now -- I hope that I have pondered morphing into a few helpful words rather than into overwhelming lists of do's and don'ts."

My purpose in structuring the three statements quoted above is to emphasize the basics of Christian belief and deemphasize **unlimited doctrines and limitless lists of "believe this" vs. "don't believe that."**

Obviously, that which emphasizes the basics of Christian belief for me will not do so for others. Likewise, the doctrines and lists that enhance Christian beliefs for others may be enigmas to me.

It is stressful to me to conjecture that Christianity has lost sight of its primary purpose which is that of all religions – to be Response-Able to (their) God's Grace* and to be responsible to/for humanity's compassion.

My response to both "No" perspectives remains the same as it was in the concluding paragraph of Blog 58.

"No matter how one believes the Christian Belief System was designed and delivered, by God or by humankind, if examined adequately, the System includes enough contradictions that it cannot be ruled infallible and it excludes enough humans that it cannot be judged compassionate.

Either way morphing is essential."

* Grace is God's business and "what God does is God's business."

(To quote Sally)

62. Another Crossroad.

In a previous book "A Belief System from Beyond the Box" I described a crossroad within my spiritual journey wherein I faced the choice of believing in the Comprehensible God of the Bible Verse, as a *Climate of Infallibilities*; or in the Incomprehensible God of the Universe, as an **Atmosphere of Possibilities**.

Here I would reference Blog 33. "And Here I Digress." That blog describes the inception and structuring of The Fortnightly Innominate Society. This Society of four retirees has met faithfully on the second and fourth Fridays of each month since February, 2010 and shows no signs of lapsing. The group has discussed innumerable topics from A to Z (e.g. from studying Advocates for progress to investigating the Zanies who spread fear of change). With a topic selected, the group spends time defining all aspects of that specific topic - including Advocates for possibilities and Zanies spreading fear.

No subject is off limits to the Innominates and no challenges are taken personally. Recently the topic "anthropomorphic concepts of God" popped up and I glibly offered my "crossroad" metaphor described in the opening paragraph above - of this Blog 62.

One of my fellow Innominates asked casually. "How long ago was it that you faced this crossroad and how do you now explain an Incomprehensible God to me?"

My answer to the first question as to timing has been given in Blog 59. There I stated that my earliest, serious, doubting/searching came when I was exposed to the persuasion of some that Christianity is not a religion but the only unique, sacred connection to the Transcendent. This selfish, exclusionary concept is absolutely counter to my later conviction that God is Grace and when the human is response-able to that Grace, that response is transformed into responsible compassion for the dignity and worth of all humanity.

As I have thought more deeply into my fellow Innominate's question, I find another crossroad. Do I trudge ahead on a solo road to morphing Christianity (the Church) expressing my personal solutions, or do I turn onto a road where there are communal solutions? I choose the communal road.

Earlier I gave copies of my book to some persons who appear to me to be thinking into their spiritual journeys as a part of their aging process. Not all of these persons are of one mind on the matter. They do display the one prerequisite essential to the communal road – they demonstrate compassion in their lives.

I shall ask a number of these persons whether they **agree** on a scale of zero to +5 (strongly agree) that Christianity must morph to survive, OR **disagree** on a scale of zero to −5 (strongly disagree) that Christianity must morph to survive.

When in doubt – conduct a survey.

Therefore I am going to take a rest from blogging while I conduct and tabulate such a study. I'll be in touch when I am back.

63. I Am Back!

Several events/concerns have deterred me but I finally return carrying an important, albeit small, armload of statistics. My first concern was designing a survey that could secure accurate data. I wanted to question a group of persons who understood what they were being questioned about. I wanted to survey persons capable of thinking beyond the box. I did not profile prospective recipients as to their belief systems or their "religions." I do not even know what churches some of them attend, in fact some may not qualify as "religious" or "Christians," in the delimiting definitions held by some "too" religious folks.

I just know all of them as friends with cognitive, social and compassionate skills that I judge to be beyond the average (and beyond what society has chosen to designate as "the box."). I had given a copy of the book I recently authored, "A Belief System from Beyond the Box" to some of these folks who live in my retirement community. Thus, survey forms could be distributed and returned anonymously through the postage-free, community mail system. In light of a low budget project I decided, after the fact, that the 20 books I had already distributed would constitute a good sampling, especially since a single book to some couples gave me a return of two questionnaires for one book.

The Survey was simple and direct:

Christianity must morph to Survive -		
Disagree	Christianity as is	Agree
Strongest (E)	(is)	Strongest (5)
E D C B A	**OK**	**1 2 3 4 5**

Instructions: Please circle only one item, e.g. **one letter, one numeral or OK.**
"My reading of the book 'A Belief System from Beyond the Box' on a completion scale of 0% to 100% would fall at _____%."

Anonymity was asked for but a few submitted comments. I can recognize four persons only, who signed questionnaires, and their comments do not skew the study. They shall remain unidentifiable beyond me.

To the recipients of the 20 books distributed I later sent 27 questionnaires. I received back 24. (Which I understand from those in the survey trade is a remarkable return.)

A Tally of the Returns:

4 responders circled **OK (as is).**

17 persons circled numerals (Agree), 2 persons circled letters (Disagree). One person agreed but circled no item.

Below: See letters/numbers circled with % read:

0% read - one person circled **1**

0% read – one person circled **C**

20% read – one person circled **5**

30% read – one person circled **C**

40 % read – one person circled **5**

45% read – one person circled **2**

75% read – one person circled **5**

80% read – one person stated, "church changing now" - **no item** circled.

85% read – one person circled **4**

100% read – three persons circled **3**
100% read – three persons circled **4**
100% read – two persons circled **5**

Observations:

1. One who disagreed strongly at **E** read **0%** of the book. One who disagreed at the **C** level read **30%** of the book.
2. All four who failed to note % of book read circled **OK** (as is).
3. 18 of the 24 returned questionnaires agreed with the premise that "Christianity must morph to survive."
4. I assure the readership that there was no intent in the distribution of the books to skew the results of a survey. The books were given long before the idea of a survey came to me.

I am aware this is a rudimentary, non-scientific survey full of variables with little chance to be a voice in the noisy gaggle of "theological truths" emanating from established Christian Circles. However this experience, with these few insightful people, convinces me that ever expanding numbers of response-able Christian Believers recognize that their beliefs must morph if Christianity is to be responsible *to* the Incomprehensible God of the Universe and *for* the communal dignity and worth of Christians in comprehensible humanity.

64. Back to What?

It was very early Monday Morning, May 2, 2011 when I put the finishing touches to the "I Am Back" blog (# 63.) that will publish May 4. Then I went to the Exercise Room to do my normal stint on the machines.

I turned on Cable TV News to learn that the almost decade of searching for Osama bin Laden had ended in a raid and his death. How should my humanness react to the death of another human responsible for the deaths of thousands of humans? Should my directives come from an Infallible Holy Book that frequently describes its God as demanding the indiscriminate slaying of thousands of humans?

Later that Monday my good friend Bill sent me an article by a seminary professor asking what the church can do to eliminate the image some laity hold that too many pastors lack humility? The same church, incidentally, which in too many instances plants and nurtures "only way to salvation" seeds in its pastors? How can pastors be humble when they have been "called" by God to show parishioners the only way to salvation.

Two dilemmas in one day!

As I have cultivated these two very different matters in my mind I am surprised to find them emerging as similar sprouts from my religious roots.

In the death of bin Laden, Christian religiosity side steps moral behavior within humanity and goes directly to theistic judgment within deity. "What would Jesus have done?"

In the deficiency of clerical humility, Christian religiosity side steps prudent behavior within humanity and misinterprets the term "call" as a theistic directive.

In both instances traditional Christianity confuses religious behavior with moral behavior and thus conflates both religion and morality.

Periodically, as I impose the philosophies of these blogs on the realities of life, I am forced to pause and review the words of Holmes Rolston III as found in the book, "Genes, Genesis and God" -- to get my bearings.

> "The divine spirit is the giver of life, pervasively present over the millennia. God is the atmosphere of possibilities, the metaphysical environment, in, with, and under first the natural and later also the cultural environment, luring the Earthen histories upslope."

The two emergent cognitive sprouts as applied to my two dilemmas:
A. Osama bin Laden's death.

Death comes to us all. Is Osama bin Laden's deep-six now more Earth beneficial than live capture and subsequent punishment?

He is dead. Are circulated post-death pictures necessary - or appropriate?

B. Humility.

I find humility comes easier all the time as one discovers more and more deficits requiring humility.

Also - I discover my responses to God come easier if God is the Atmosphere of Possibilities luring me upslope in the Universe, rather than an anthropomorphic icon in the Bible Verse directing my status quo.

65. Analysis Paralysis.

"The term "analysis paralysis" or "paralysis of analysis" refers to over-analyzing (or over-thinking) a situation, so that a decision or action is never taken, in effect paralyzing the outcome." Wikipedia.

I find myself in analysis paralysis as I study the tiny armload of data just recently acquired from a poll based on the statement, "Christianity must morph to survive."

In my observations 1 and 2, listed again below, am I being overly defensive as I point out the six responders who do not agree with the premise, "Christianity must morph to survive?" I fear I am. In retrospect, observations 1 and 2 could be construed as subtle attempts to substantiate the value of reading the book – not as responses to the matter of morphing Christianity.

1. One who disagreed strongly at **E** read **0**% of the book. One who disagreed at the **C** level read **30**% of the book.
2. All four, who failed to note a % of the book read, circled **OK** (as is).
3. 18 of the 24 returned questionnaires agreed with the premise that "Christianity must morph to survive."
4. I assure the readership that there was no intent in the

distribution of the books to skew the results of a survey. The books were given long before the idea of a survey came to me.

Observation 4 is true but is superfluous to the intent of the survey and thus has no value as data.

That leaves observation 3 as the only valuable data relative to morphing Christianity. That is sufficient for me. There are *tons* of data available to substantiate this meager study. The paralysis of analysis is not in collecting or studying the data – it is in applying it. The tons already collected are not being applied any more quickly than my meager armload.

I am well aware that my sample of 27 persons questioned, yielding 24 responses with 18 agreeing that Christianity needs to morph, is not remotely representative of the statistics for the all of Christianity. But it presents one unequivocal positive. I know all 24 persons who answered the survey as persons and not as statistics. I know who four are because they signed their questionnaires. I have no idea who the other 20 are, as related to the questionnaires, nor would I even attempt to guess which category, "agree, disagree or OK (as is)" they would choose. The normal contacts between residents in a retirement community have not given me such insights into their belief systems.

Understanding or being friends with specific others only because we think or believe alike is risky to the whole of society. It is an especial risk in churches as examples of Christianity. We need only explore schisms in congregations as cases in point.

Christianity has existed as a religion for some 2000 years. Its adherents have done some marvelously good acts as well as some terribly bad acts in the name of Christianity. To affirm its religiosity Christianity continues to search back all the way to some unknown span of time when Logos mythically attached divine connectors to the receptors empowering reason within developing humanity. There is risk in searching back so far. The longer a religion has existed the less excuse it has for not exhibiting maturity (spelled c-o-m-p-a-s-s-i-o-n) toward the rest of humanity.

I repeat the closing paragraph of Blog 63: I am aware this is a rudimentary, non-scientific survey full of variables with little chance to be a voice in the noisy gaggle of "theological truths" emanating from established Christian circles. However, this survey experience with these few insightful people, convinces me that ever expanding numbers of Christians recognize that their beliefs must morph *in a steady though cautious manner* if Christianity is to be response-able to the Incomprehensible God of the Universe and join in the communal dignity and worth of all who comprise comprehensible humanity.

66. The response came.

Yes, the response came. I had expected it since soon after I posted Blog 64.

In that blog, dealing with the death of Osama bin Laden, I ducked the issue of my responsibility as an American citizen for the handling of his capture – or his death. I left my decision on the matter as a question in blog 64.

"A. Osama bin Laden's death.

Death comes to us all. Is Osama bin Laden's deep-six now more Earth beneficial than it would be if it came later, e.g. after trial and punishment?

He is dead. Are circulated post-death pictures necessary - or appropriate?"

The response from the reader of my blog was simple and direct:

"Suppose you are the citizen of the United States directing the bin Laden capture or kill mission; what are your instructions to our team of US Navy Seals?"

Of course my responder didn't mean a "complete" plan. He is aware that I don't even know how to start a helicopter. What he is asking is – "Do we take bin Laden dead? or alive? If alive where do we take him? If dead what do we do with the body? If dead what constitutes proof? How do you balance the manifold: world security (law and justice), US security (law and justice), patriotism, moral and religious principles?"

I have given much thought to this matter - not morbid thought. Rather soul-searching, human being thought, US citizen thought - plus concern for human dignity and worth, for our country, for our Commander-in-Chief, for all involved in the mission and for **all** suffering its repercussions.

Two rules hold for all actions in a war:

1. All events twist and turn second by second.
2. All results will be twisted and turned later - by all involved - and by too many uninvolved.

I believe that valid cases can be built for alive and for dead (either/or). The case rests on past history and also future safety. This is especially true since raid materials recovered show that bin Laden was planning future deaths of more innocents.

Where to take a live bin Laden became a moot question.

The general consensus is that proper respect and decorum were observed in the burial of the body.

I trust DNA testing to prove the body to be that of Osama bin Laden.

I trust the current policy on the viewing of the death pictures. I trust our leaders to use such evidence for authentication not pontification or retribution.

I am well aware that many will wonder why I spent time thinking and writing on this matter when to them it is black and white.

Reports convince me that the leaders of our nation, the planners of the bin Laden Mission, spent tortuous hours justifying the risks to our personnel and the impact of the mission's methodology on world opinion of our country's treatment of justice and law.

All of us as citizens are a part of that justice and law. That is why I've given a lot of thought to this matter. I see it as inextricably entangled with our religious belief systems.

My next blog will approach "WWJD." -- What Would Jesus Do?

67. "WWJD."

"What would Jesus do?"

In Blog 64 I describe how early morning CNN on May 2, 2011 brought me the news that Osama bin Laden had been apprehended and killed. As my mind fumbled through what my human law and justice reaction should be to this circumstance, my belief system calmly expanded the scope of inquiry to provide me today's oft quoted words, **"What would Jesus have done?"**

Many years ago I was the facilitator in a course dealing with the "Reformed Tradition" for a class in our Presbytery's Certified Lay Preacher (now Lay Pastor) curriculum. One of the class members was a senior-aged lady with a sturdy "Old Time Religion" belief system. Sally utilized reformed theology to what she felt was its effective level, but when she found herself in an untenable corner her theism would step front and center and her solution was, "What God does is God's Business." On the morning of May 2, 2011 I could hear Sally's unequivocal words in my mind – "God gave bin Laden exactly what he deserved." These words define theism in practice.

Here is theism defined by my computer's dictionary:

> theism, noun
> belief in the existence of a god or gods, esp. in one god as creator of the universe, intervening in it and sustaining a personal relation to his creatures.

The theism that I struggle with constantly is just as deeply rooted in my belief system as Sally's was in hers, but it is subtler. Perhaps hers was one edition earlier than mine. Perhaps hers was the Old Testament Jehovahean variety while mine is the New Testament Christusean variety.

Perhaps that is why she would state emphatically, "God gave bin Laden exactly what he deserved," while I would muse more thoughtfully, "What would Jesus have done?"

The worst "perhaps" of all is this one – perhaps the traditions and teachings of Christianity have permitted (encouraged?) me to structure my belief systems on theistic foundations.

Just as I was coming to finalize this Blog 67, Serendipity and the e-mail brought me this week's John Shelby Spong Essay. Here is his concluding question and answer.

Question:

It has been our privilege to hear your lectures at Highlands, and they are always exciting and provocative. We feel your message to the world is "Copernican" in scope and potential. We have read all your books through the years, but I don't recall you ever addressing the idea of the concept of the "Origin of God" in humanity's time. Do you have a hunch or idea or knowledge of when this concept entered the human drama?

Answer:

Dear Friends,

Thank you for your letter. I have addressed that subject in my book *Eternal Life: A New Vision* but perhaps not in the way you might expect.

I do not believe the human brain can speak to the origin of God. We can speak to the origin of the human concept of God, but that is something quite different. That idea I believe is born in the moment that self-consciousness breaks through consciousness in human development. That human idea almost always portrays God as external to this world, invisible or located beyond the limits of our sight, which is what "above the sky" means. This deity is then endowed with supernatural power and is said to be ready to come to our aid if we worship properly, obey God's rules and pray sufficiently hard. It is what I have called a "theistic" concept of God. Theism is a definition of God from the childhood of our humanity and ultimately it needs to be abandoned. Most of us cling to it tenaciously because we do not know any other way to envision the holy.

68. Above the Sky.

Early this morning, June 1, 2011, United States Spaceship Endeavor returned safely to Earth from an eight day docking with the International Space Station – "above the sky."

I am tempted to launch into a typical waste of verbiage - waste from the perspective of the writer as well as the reader. It is obvious that early humans trying to explain the nature of God, would describe the incomprehensible as existing above the sky beyond the comprehensible environs of human life while still controlling the comprehensible actions and/or mental processes of that life. Why do humans persist in expanding this seminal thesis into theism with the hope of rendering the incomprehensible tangible and knowable?

Humans have chosen to turn a. God's incomprehensible existence and b. God's incomprehensible nature into humanity's two greatest needs for words, words, words, ad infinitum. Words can describe and explain what the human can comprehend. Words cannot describe nor explain that which is incomprehensible.

It occurs to me that the human should transfer its limited comprehension from struggling futilely with God's nature and existence to struggling with the dilemmas of its own nature and existence.

I shall approach what I consider to be the two greatest human dilemmas after sharing an anecdote.

In earlier blogs I have referred to the Fortnightly Innominate Society. We four old geezers are plugging along stronger than ever meeting the Second and Fourth Friday of the month from 9:30 a.m. to 10:30 a.m. (or so). During the Easter Season we chose to devote two sessions to the Atonement. We were free to research wherever and however we pleased and bring whatever opinions we wanted to share to the plenary meetings.

We arrived at the first of these two sessions suffering from overwhelming atonement fatigue. Amazingly we had developed similar conclusions.

I shall share my personal conclusions. Scholars have taken this concept (atonement) from the past, actually a "beyond the sky" concept, suffocated it with long words denoting contrived categories of atonement to the point of theism where there is no possibility of help for daily living from a plethora of atonement concepts.

Here is a vignette of how I see some within Christianity using Atonement as a tool of theism within daily living:

Scene: Street of a small town.

Church going resident meets new person just moved to town.

Resident: "Heard you had just moved to our town. Welcome. Hope you are looking for a Christian Church Home."

Newcomer: "Well, yes, we are."

Resident: "We welcome all folks with their personal beliefs to our church. Let me be the first to invite you to church - the New Testament Church on the corner of Hope and Faith where we worship Christ every Sunday at 10:30 a.m. as the only way to Salvation and the way to sure Atonement of our sins."

Note: The Resident would have used the term Substitutionary Atonement instead of sure Atonement but the longer word slipped his mind for the moment.

I apologize to all readers who disagree but our Innominate Society's solution was to cancel the second session on atonement and devote it to another topic.

With the anecdote and vignette behind me I shall soon return to what I consider to be the two ultimate human dilemmas. These are:

How can we be responsible to all of nature including human beings, and how can we be response-able to whatever *metaphysical force* gives purpose to all of existence?

69. Inherent.

It is the inherent nature of humans to believe that some metaphysical force renders purpose to existence. Futile chaos erupts when humans design myriad, competitive comprehensions to explain the nature of that force.

Yes – theology as a systemic field still attempts to comprehend the nature of that which too many scholars of theology refuse to recognize as incomprehensible.

Yes – theology as a systemic field can and does create futile chaos.

The chaos of theology can range from sophomoric debates to horrific wars. Although the range of the chaos is becoming more limited the outcome is invariably futility. In fact the end points of discussions or wars dealing with the incomprehensible can only be futility.

Unfortunately theology, to fulfill its name, struggles with the incomprehensible by producing suffocating masses of words - comprehensible words plus torrents of specialized, jargon words, e.g. Summa Theologica. Theological concepts germinate seminal words that sustain those concepts as they categorically germinate more words to produce perpetual cycles of jargon.

It has been a breath of fresh air to me to read the incontrovertible wisdom of Holmes Rolston III's observation in "Genes, Genesis and God" that "God is the Atmosphere of Possibilities luring human histories upslope." I can add that to my belief statement.

Within that atmosphere of possibilities I am currently reading the book "Christianity, The First Three Thousand Years" by Diarmaid MacCulloch. Therein I have already acquired another breath of fresh air and I am a mere 488 pages into this 1161 page treasure trove. I'll take some space in this blog to report that breath and report others later as I discover them.

MacCulloch is a professor of History at Oxford University. To introduce his background and his belief system I shall present a short excerpt from page 11 of this Introduction to the book.

"I was brought up in the presence of the Bible, and I remember what it was like to hold a dogmatic position on the statements of Christian belief. I would now describe myself as a candid friend of Christianity. I still appreciate the seriousness which a religious mentality brings to the mystery and misery of human existence and I appreciate the solemnity of religious liturgy as a way of confronting these problems. I live with the puzzle of wondering how something so apparently crazy can be so captivating to millions of other members of my species. It is in part to answer that question for myself that I seek out the history of this world faith, alongside those of humankind's countless other expressions of religious belief and practice. Maybe some familiar with theological jargon will with charity regard this as an apophatic form of the Christian faith."

Then to get to MacColloch's definition of apophatic I was obliged to read on to page 439. There I found his definition of apophatic.

"Dionysian theology was also Neoplatonic in its view of the cosmos as a series of hierarchies; not as an obstacle to God, but as the means of uniting the remoteness and unknowableness of God with the knowable particularity of lower creation, just as courtiers might be intermediaries for humble people to approach a monarch. God could be known in precisely opposite ways: by what could not be said about him (the 'apophatic' view of God) and what could be affirmed about him (the kataphatic view.)"

(Blogger's note: The Dionysian theory states that the "unknowable" God could be "known" [?] in precisely opposite ways which to me are not "ways" but unprovable, human jargon concepts - apophatic and kataphatic)

Thus I see MacCulloch wondering, "how something [Christianity] so apparently crazy can be so captivating to millions of other members of my species," could perhaps be converted via jargon "to an apophatic form of the Christian faith," [by his (MacCulloch's) extensive historical research.]

Let's see?

MacColluch says –
"I would now describe myself as a candid friend of Christianity."
(Blogger note – This could fit into my belief system.)

MacCulloch says --

"I live with the puzzle of wondering how something so apparently crazy can be so captivating to millions of other members of my species."

(Blogger note – This could also fit into my belief system but I might soften the word crazy to avoid some modern day equivalent of "being burned at the stake.")

70. Two Dilemmas.

How can we be responsible to all of nature including human beings, and how can we be response-able to whatever *metaphysical force* gives purpose to all of existence?

These are dissimilar, stand-alone dilemmas – not similar dilemmas vying with each other for priority status.

1. How are we responsible to comprehensible humanity? via human-*ism*?
2. How are we response-able to the incomprehensible metaphysical force?

    via as many *–isms* as there are theological concepts of God?

I do not mean to brush past dilemma #1. but this blog series continually cites sources of help in that area. The defining word is compassion. Karen Armstrong's writings and the Charter for Compassion are basic. Robert Wright's section on Moral Imagination in "The Evolution of God" is another basic approach. John Shelby Spong's concepts help frequently. On and on other mind-sets contribute.

Christianity, and its institutional church system, prove consistently that both can and do present the means for humans to be responsible to and for one another across this Earth. Then why is Christianity in the U.S. and many other places losing members and influence? Sadly to say I fear that Diarmaid MacCulloch has his finger on the pulse of Christianity when he says, "I live with the puzzle of wondering how something so apparently crazy can be so captivating to millions of other members of my species." This is an apophatic, pertinent statement about Christianity as opposed to the kataphatic statement that was not made. That would be my paraphrase of MacCulloch, "I wonder why something so apparently useful is losing its members and influence at such an alarming rate."

This blogger offers a couple of thoughts on why Christianity today appears "so apparently crazy" to questioning members and to so many potential members but not "so apparently crazy" to captivated millions.

First - as a theological concept setting forth the nature of God, Christianity was structured in a time when very little was known about the "above the sky" nature of the universe(s). Knowledge of what is has changed but Christianity's explanatory theism has not. Once established traditional concepts change or die ever so slowly.

Second – Christianity's concept of a divine human savior predicted by Judaic scriptures from centuries of an established, bone fide, monotheistic religion was in competition with many strong religions. Christianity chose as its edge the claim that it was the only way to salvation. Saul of Tarsus and later Roman Emperor Constantine offered visions that substantiated this claim. Traditions die ever so slowly. Visions can live forever.

As I sum up the secular dilemma of humans being responsible to humans, I find that I have chosen as my solution a very comprehensible human trait – compassion.

As I sum up the dilemma of religious humans being response-able to the incomprehensible metaphysical force that gives purpose to existence, I find that too many religions claim that they are the only way to commune with that Force. These claims leave billions of fellow humans outside the bounds of compassion.

I find these words of Robert Wright (p.430, The Evolution of God) speak profoundly to both of these dilemmas:

"And like it or not the social system to be saved is a global one. Any religion whose prerequisites for individual salvation don't conduce to the salvation of the whole world is a religion whose time has passed."

71. Review Time.

Periodically I scan through this string of blogs to see if they are neat and tidy with no dangling participles or concepts. I have just done this and I do find some dangling deficits.

I demean jargon then jerry-build concepts full of it. I become so pleased with some phrases that I abuse them into clichés. I am expert at converting aptitude to platitude. I berate theism then create new examples of it.

In spite of these weaknesses I still recognize that I am at risk of leaving a partial description of theism as a dangling deficit. So let's start here with the basics.

I promise to avoid the thousands of jargon words that litter the field of theology. For example we have struggled in a recent blog with apophatic and kataphatic and I ask the reader – do you feel any more capable of understanding the nature of God than you did before these two words came into your life?

As we approach the concept of theism we have no choice but to expand the discussion to include the words deism and atheism.

> deism - noun belief in the existence of a supreme being, specifically of a creator who does not intervene in the universe.

> theism – noun belief in the existence of a god or gods, especially belief in one god as creator of the universe intervening in it and sustaining a personal relation to his creation.

> atheism – noun the theory or belief that God does not exist.

Immediately we find ourselves on a misadventure. It is improper for those who belief in deism not to be faced with counterparts if those who belief in theism are faced with atheists. I do not find the word adeist in my dictionary. Out of fairness I shall coin it. Please remember you first saw it here.

One more diversion and we are ready to go. Some folks would have us include the terms gnostic and agnostic (gnosticism and agnosticism). To me these terms go beyond the basic needs in our spiritual lives and teeter on the edge of jargon. I'll leave the use of these words to others.

OK – now we have three more words to help us understand theism –

deism, adeism, theism, atheism as nouns (deistic, adeistic, theistic, atheistic as adjectives).

To avoid theological jargon I shall define these four words using modern anecdotal, jargon-free terms:

deist - believes that God created everything including autos and large mall parking lots and has retired to his throne with no intention of directing anyone to a parking space on a crowded day.

adeist – believes there is no God and anyway it's better to take the bus to the mall.

theist - believes God designs autos and mall parking lots and if he flatters God enough, and prays hard enough, God, although far away on his throne, will still direct the theist to a needed parking space.

atheist – the word adeist renders this word, atheist, archaic since adeist more accurately takes over atheist's old meaning - "the theory or belief that God does not exist."

As this blog series reveals I am making strenuous efforts to transition from being a theist to being a possibilitist. What is a possibilitist?

possibilitist – noun one who believes that God is the Atmosphere of Possibilities in which autos and parking lots can exist and if humans need and secure an auto and search diligently enough they can find a place to park it. This Possibility God does not sit on a remote throne but is an everywhere, brilliant atmosphere, luring all humans out of the dark and upslope to the light. (ALL humans – not just some that believe specific tenets and doctrines, stored for centuries in crumbling, traditional boxes.)

72. Words, Words, Words.

It is obvious, from my last few blogs, that I am adverse to large, contrived, coined, jargon-like words that dominate the field of theology. It is no wonder to me why we common humans wander aimlessly in the vast theological jumble (jungle?).

Actually I love words – the functional, melodious ones that are not too ostentatious, contrived or obtuse. Immediately I can think of a word that has intrigued me since my initial contact with it – existential. The understandable definition of the word is:

existential - adjective - of or related to existence.

The word existential was not a part of my growing up. It came to me at about midlife – and then indirectly. At some point about half way through the 20th Century theologians rediscovered and flexed the words of Soren Kierkegaard concerning belief of the unprovable as requiring a "leap of faith." The words existential, existentialist and existentialism were soon a part of such discussions.

Further research indicates that the word existentialism seems to have been coined by the French philosopher Gabriel Marcel in the mid-1940s and has never become fully understood since its birth.

As a starting point in preparation for this blog I went to the Stanford Encyclopedia of Philosophy to study existential and its ism. No aspersions on the Encyclopedia, but a few hours of reading proved that I was not the audience this material on existentialism had been produced for.

The next research choice, Wikipedia, was in my league and I'll quote a section to get us started:

"A **leap of faith**, in its most commonly used meaning, is the act of believing in or accepting something intangible or unprovable, or without empirical evidence.[1] It is an act commonly associated with religious belief as many religions consider faith to be an essential element of piety.

The phrase is commonly attributed to Søren Kierkegaard; however, he himself never used the term, as he referred to a leap as a leap to faith. A leap of faith according to Kierkegaard involves circularity insofar as a leap is made by faith.[2] In his book The Concept of Anxiety, he describes the core part of the leap of faith, the leap. He does this using the famous story of Adam and Eve, particularly Adam's qualitative leap into sin. Adam's leap signifies a change from one quality to another, mainly the quality of possessing no sin to the quality of possessing sin. Kierkegaard maintains that the transition from one quality to another can take place only by a "leap" (Thomte 232). When the transition happens, one moves directly from one state to the other, never possessing both qualities."

The immediate concern that I have with Kierkegaard's reasoning is that he would disavow the statement "Christianity must morph to survive." Per his concept "Christianity must leap to survival" because transitioning (possessing two qualities simultaneously) is not possible. At the moment I am not prompted to forsake morphing or prepared to reject leaping. My Presbyterian core, moderation in all things, suggests that both paths have value and melding the two has merit.

I do not intend to leave the words existential, existentialism and existentialist as dangling deficits. My current definition of existential is:

> existential - adjective What was, may have been. What is, may be. What tradition predicts will be, may not.

Robert Fulgham treated knowledge judiciously in his book - "Everything I Needed to Know I Learned in Kindergarten." He states later that he saw a bumper sticker that lends balance to his writings:

"Don't Believe All You Think"

Plaques with these words could be appropriate in some theologian's studies - especially those who overuse words we didn't learn in kindergarten,

73. Don't Believe All You think.

Of course this is a take off on - "Don't believe all you hear."

My problem is that I have not utilized either saying adequately to grant me the wisdom to be gained from following these two sensible admonitions.

I shall return to a theme I explored long ago in this blog series, "Do some believers take their specific religions too seriously." I'll expand the theme. "Do some specific religious entities take themselves too seriously?"

My answer to both questions is yes - if persons or religious entities believe they possess the only path to the metaphysical force that renders purpose to existence.

Christianity exists today because it has not permitted its members to believe all they thought. Christianity is at risk today because it has demanded that its members believe too much that has become outmoded through eons wherein humankind's secular knowledge and mores change day by day. Need I mention former years of supporting slavery and present years of denying innumerable rights to unimaginable millions of humans?

Diarmaid MacCulloch has his finger on the erratic pulse of Christianity when he says, "I live with the puzzle of wondering how something so apparently crazy can be so captivating to millions of other members of my species."

Out of deference to my fear of punishment at the stake, I would reduce the word "crazy" to "suspect."

74. Existential – A Reprise.

On my birthday one day in January several years ago my wife, Elinor, gave me a small, neatly wrapped gift. It was an esthetic ceramic plaque with a leather thong for hanging. Elinor was aware of a bonding phrase that had arisen within a deep friendship between our Pastor Bill and myself. This ceramic plaque carried the phrase, "Thou shalt not whine."

I had to wait until October to regift the same plaque forward to Bill for his birthday. A few days later I found the plaque neatly installed just above the light switch in the Church Parlor. In proper hands a good phrase can go far.

As I prepared the blog dealing with Soren Kierkegaard's famous attributed quote, "Leap of faith," which he always used as a, "Leap to faith," it came to me that it was time for me to desist from explaining why I am leaping **to** a new concept of my faith - lest it break my affirmative response to, "Thou shalt not whine," It is time to shift to thinking about what I am leaping to.

Let's return for the moment to what I left with the reader as my definition of existential - a reprise, if you will:

> existential - adjective What was, may have been. What is, may be. What tradition predicts will be, may not.

An expanded version:

> What was, may have been. It may not have been. My whining OR actions won't change either.

> What is, may be. It may not be. My whining won't change either. My actions can change BOTH.

> What tradition predicts will be, may not. Some think* - it is possible to leap TO a new spirituality – others think those who believe this are befuddled.

> * e.g. Following Kierkegaard's "Leap TO faith" concept, I believe that I can, "Leap to a new spirituality and escape my old theism."

75. Morph – A Reprise.

Much earlier I softened the oft quoted admonition – "Christianity must change or it will die," to my softer version – "Christianity must morph to survive." The latter phrase has appeared so frequently in these pages that it has unintentionally attained mantra status.

In Blog 72: Words, Words, Words -- I subjected "morph" to Kierkegaard's concept – "leap to faith." Here is that paragraph.

"The immediate concern that I have with Kierkegaard's reasoning is that he would disavow the statement "Christianity must morph to survive." Per his concept "Christianity must leap to survival" because transitioning (possessing two qualities simultaneously) is not possible. At the moment I am not prompted to forsake morphing or prepared to reject leaping. My Presbyterian core, moderation in all things, suggests that both paths have value and melding the two has merit."

Yes, I believe melding does have merit and here is a suggestion I offer for consideration:

If Christianity discards its old religiosity and leaps to a new spirituality, it can survive.

religiosity -- noun – state of being excessively religious.

spiritual – adjective – of, relating to, or affecting the human spirit.

spirituality -- noun

I fear that Christianity maintains concepts that are justifiably labeled old religiosities at a time when so many are searching for new spiritualities that will render morphing possible.

A leap to religion is not a foreordained leap to faith. Religion must include faith but too often religiosity can weaken, even smother, faith. John Shelby Spong refers to this smothering in the following quote that I used earlier in Blog. 62:

"I do not believe the human brain can speak to the origin

of God. We can speak to the origin of the human concept of God, but that is something quite different. That idea I believe is born in the moment that self-consciousness breaks through consciousness in human development. That human idea almost always portrays God as external to this world, invisible or located beyond the limits of our sight, which is what "above the sky" means. This deity is then endowed with supernatural power and is said to be ready to come to our aid if we worship properly, obey God's rules and pray sufficiently hard. It is what I have called a "theistic" concept of God. Theism is a definition of God from the childhood of our humanity and ultimately it needs to be abandoned. Most of us cling to it tenaciously because we do not know any other way to envision the holy."

76. A Change of Direction.

In Blog 3. I shared the story of the church board that refused to permit the burial in its cemetery, the only one in town, of a man who froze to death one night on his way home from a saloon. The board's stated reason – "After all, this was a man who had chosen to be the town drunk." I would term this position religiosity.

Through blog after blog of accounts of traditionalism, anthropomorphism, theism **and** religiosity I have elaborated reasons why, in my mind, Christianity must morph to survive.

I do not claim that all my verbiage on why Christianity must morph should be accepted. I realize it is my opinion, and per Patrick Daniel Moynihan's famous quote – "Every one is entitled to his own opinion, but not his own facts."

This quote was attributed to Moynihan as a 1994 remark on Radio WNBC New York to an electoral opponent. Incidentally, the identical quote is attributed to James R. Schlesinger in 1973 Congressional testimony. Which are we to believe as the original?

I do not believe all I think. Long ago, before I discovered Holmes Rolston III's Atmosphere of Possibilities, I had concluded that the Universal Laws of Nature, stable enough to support human existence, were merely a subset of a metaphysical force that renders purpose to the total of existence. I do believe this metaphysical force exists. I do not believe that I can comprehend it nor can I prove it by naming it God and expounding on its nature in kataphatic or apophatic jargon, although I sometimes appear to.

In the previous blog I ended with John Shelby Spong's statement on theism:

> 'Theism is a definition of God from the childhood of our humanity and ultimately it needs to be abandoned. Most of us cling to it tenaciously because we do not know any other way to envision the holy."

Humans now have learned that specific DNAs, under instructions from unique genetic codes, produce replicable life. I am perfectly content to assume that there is some metaphysical force which I cannot comprehend rendering purpose to this existential process and to my potential for leaping. If one wants to take a holy leap to theism or anthropomorphism as parts of Christian belief then, to use the candid words of MacCulloch, this is further than my evolving understanding will permit me to leap. I am perfectly happy to take up residence in the atmosphere of possibilities.

On occasion snippets of theism drift into my mind. More and more I just permit them to float on through. I do not encourage them to attach to my belief system.

77. Is Prayer Theism?

Perhaps the prior question should be – Is worship theism? Unfortunately, it can be. We Christians worship God because we are thankful and because we believe God can help us. Because we think, we believe that God thinks in similar fashion. Thus we transfer to that which we worship our human "power of thinking." That is theism. What if we expand our concept of God to an incomprehensible metaphysical force that renders purpose to the entirety of existence? This is something totally different from a "being that thinks." Granted we should be thankful for the all of existence, but not to a directive God that we would ask to break the universal laws of that existence to respond to our worshipful pleadings to solve our individual needs. Again, that is theism.

I am trying - but prayer still drifts into my mind as snippets of theism. Our youngest of six children died in 2010 from breast cancer at age 49 - at the pinnacle of a wonderfully creative life. The snippets became crushing weights. So now where was my incomprehensible, metaphysical force that renders purpose to the entirety of existence? It was with us but it did not come to us as a theistic, comforting, benevolent God "taking Stacey home." It came to us as thankfulness that we had the possibility to know such a remarkable person for 49 years.

My prayers are not to realize theistic benefits – rather, they are thanks for the viable spirituality that empowers me to recognize the incomprehensible Atmosphere of Possibilities.

78. Can Creeds and Confessions Be Theistic?

The Scriptural basis of Judeo-Christianity was spoken, then written and finally canonized as the portrayal of a Directive God in relationship with specific humans over a restricted frame of time. These scriptural accounts were prepared by humans having insights compatible with the cultures and knowledge of their various, extant times. There were of course humans within this process who realized that there was "a something that gave purpose to what they viewed as the universe." It was most natural that this something was an anthropomorphic being directing earthly affairs from "somewhere beyond the sky." (Probably from a throne?)

The scriptures should not be faulted because they are theistic. We humans of today should be faulted because we still accept a theism that was essential to those who structured it in another time. We should be faulted further because we accept the tradition that subsequent concepts, creeds and confessions are to be based on these theistic scriptures.

As Part 1 of the Constitution of the Presbyterian Church (USA) this denomination enfolds its several Confessional Documents into a Book of Confessions. I have read these documents plus considerable critiquing of the same. In all reverence I must offer that much of the content could be classified as apophatic and kataphatic redundancies of a theological nature which are stored in the box that I must leap beyond to find a viable spirituality that I can utilize and fulfill in my every-day existence.

Just now the PCUSA Presbyteries are voting whether to add another Confession to the Book of Confessions. This is the Belhar Confession as described by the following Prologue:

The Belhar Confession has its roots in the struggle against apartheid in Southern Africa. This "outcry of faith" and "call for faithfulness and repentance" was first drafted in 1982 by the Dutch Reformed Mission Church (DRMC) under the leadership of Allan Boesak. The DRMC took the lead in declaring that apartheid constituted a status confessionis in which the truth of the gospel was at stake.

The Dutch Reformed Mission Church formally adopted the Belhar Confession in 1986. It is now one of the "standards of unity" of the new Uniting Reformed Church in Southern Africa (URCSA). Belhar's theological confrontation of the sin of racism has made possible reconciliation among Reformed churches in Southern Africa and has aided the process of reconciliation within the nation of South Africa.

Belhar's relevance is not confined to Southern Africa. It addresses three key issues of concern to all churches: unity of the church and unity among all people, reconciliation within church and society, and God's justice. As one member of the URCSA has said, "We carry this confession on behalf of all the Reformed churches. We do not think of it as ours alone." The Belhar Confession was adopted by the RCA's 2009 General Synod. It is awaiting ratification by two-thirds of the RCA's classes, which will report their votes to General Synod 2010.

On the day of voting on the acceptance of this Belhar Confession by one PCUSA Presbytery a seminary student rose to ask the Assembly to reject the addition of the Confession. Here is a condensed version of the student's statement:

"Does this Assembly grasp how much the addition of this confession will add to the load seminary students must assimilate and be tested on as they go through their studies and ordination exams?"

Laypersons cope with the volumes of material they are asked by our denomination (PCUSA) to absorb as confessions, creeds and theological constructs. I pose this question: Does my church grasp how much the addition of this confession will add to the contents of the box that I must leap beyond to find a viable spirituality that I can utilize in fulfilling my every-day existence?

Technically an atheist is one who does not believe in a theistic (directive) God. In that usage of the word I am an atheist. One who does not believe in any God would more accurately be an adeist – but this word does not exist. In a world that is coming to be more holistic than theistic, I would offer that the metaphysical force that renders value and purpose to the all of existence is better conceptualized as the Atmosphere of Possibilities than as a Library of Theism.

79. What About Holistic Religion?

Holistic is another word that came to me later in life. As an adjective applied to the field of philosophy it refers to gathering all aspects of a premise into a whole. Holistic medicine broadens treatment beyond the physical symptoms of disease to include mental and social factors.

What about "holistic religion?" Google gave me 15,000,000 related hits. Here is Google entry #4 on the first list of 10 -

"Spiritual but not **religious**? Put 'holistic' on your census form ...www.guardian.co.uk/.../belief/.../**holistic-religious**-atheist-census - Cached

Mar 2, 2011 – William Bloom: An awareness of life's magic benefits physical and mental health – those who feel this way should speak with a coherent ..."

At the following address I met William Bloom:

http://www.google.com/search?client=safari&rls=en-us&q=holistic%20religion&ie=UTF-8&oe=UTF-8

The reader can explore William Bloom on Google. I find him a very interesting Brit Ph.D. writing this Opinion piece for the Guardian. This heading to his piece on what to tell the census taker about your religion gives insights to my question: "What about holistic religion?"

"question: What should we tell the census about our religious affiliation?

The debate between secularists and religious believers is now hopelessly out of date and obscures a much more important perspective in contemporary religious culture. This new perspective is best described as 'as spiritual but not religious', or holistic."

Here are the final paragraphs that summarize the article precisely:

"Society has moved forward. Traditional loyalties to single faiths are dissolving as, informed by multiculturalism and global awareness, people respect the positive essence of religion but want to avoid the conflict-ridden and confining superstructures.

For want of a better term, putting 'holistic' in the religion box may be the best and most hopeful signal for this census."

This blogger's Editorial Note:

I agree with William Bloom that answering "holistic" in the religion box on census forms of governments is the most accurate term for the current era.

My summation: One can leap directly to the Spiritual without struggling through the religious.

80. Alternative Religions.

The fields of Alternative Education and Alternative Medicine are growing rapidly as answers to deficits, real or imagined, in these given areas.

Somewhere in the wasteland short of fertile thoughts this one popped into my mind: "Wonder what Googling 'Alternative Religions' would yield?"

WOW! About 194,000,000 related items is all - plus listings of thousands of entities fitting the classification - Alternative Religion.

Then I tried "Alternatives to Religion" and it yielded a mere 25,900,000 results. Some of the websites offered were the same in the first groupings of 10 at each terminology although the search terms are totally different.

Of course this blog # 80 has been a diversionary exercise. Religions are the problem, thus alternative religions cannot be the solution. The disappointment risked in changing denominations or religions has been high amongst those whom I have observed trying it.

The word shrift came to my mind. I went there:

> shrift noun archaic - confession to a priest. *See also short shrift*.
> short shrift noun rapid and unsympathetic dismissal; curt treatment.

As for Alternative Religions: What about *short shrift*?
As for Alternative to Religion? What about a leap to spirituality?

81. Definitions.

Sometimes – If a word doesn't fit, don't go to another word, just go to another dictionary.

For example if I want to use the word rightness or the word righteousness per their secular contexts I can convey similar meanings. But, if I conflate righteousness to the specific meanings various religions impose, it may no longer resemble rightness. e.g. it may be more theistic than secular – more righteous than right (correct).

What does this mean? It means that it could make more sense for me to leap to rightness than to leap to a specific righteousness, i.e. a faith. Long years of observation have led me to the conclusion that religions conflate the terms righteousness, faith and belief into meanings that justify the dictums of that religion. This is a profound turning point in my search for validity in the quest of morphing Christianity.

For the present I shall restrict my observations to our Presbyterian denomination (PCUSA) in the United States. This branch of Christianity has lost half its membership in recent years. Its factions have spent hundreds of years debating peripherals e.g. "original sins, angels on pins and ordination i.e. who wins?" – as opposed to confronting its existential detractors: traditionalism, anthropomorphism, theism, religiosity, etc.

Presbyterians appear to keep hoping that the institution can correct its decline through confessions, parliamentary procedures and alterations of its Book of Order (Constitution). However increasing factionalism would appear to be trending toward probable schisms, acceleration of decline and dissolution of the institution. If Presbyterianism, or if Christianity, collapses does this mean the collapse of spirituality? Of course not. The metaphysical force that gives purpose to existence is not dependent on human institutions. Spirituality does not derive from religions. It derives from pinches of the metaphysical force within all of existence.

What is my change of direction? Christianity will not morph through parliamentary procedural events but when its adherents leap to individual basic spiritualities as opposed to a plethora of institutional, righteous ones.

82. Just By Chance

I just attended the Second Friday in August Meeting of the Innominate Society. The discussion concerned how family and society are failing the current student generation within their education – and what can we do? At the end of that topic I ventured that churches are also failing this generation within their religious experience. Another of the four Innominates asked if I might be overlooking the consistent wonders that derive from the labors of churches as I press Christianity to morph.

I later went back through these blogs to see if my writing was indeed conveying my fellow Innominate's observation of my spoken thoughts. I came upon the following in Blog 70. Two Dilemmas.

"Christianity, and its institutional church system, prove consistently that both can and do present the means for humans to be responsible to and for one another across this Earth. Then why is Christianity in the U.S. and many other places, losing members and influence? Sadly to say I fear that Diarmaid MacCulloch has his finger on the pulse of Christianity when he says, "I live with the puzzle of wondering how something so apparently crazy can be so captivating to millions of other members of my species." This is an apophatic, pertinent statement about Christianity as opposed to the kataphatic statement that was not made. That statement would be my paraphrase of MacCulloch, "I wonder why something so apparently useful is losing its members and influence at such an alarming rate."

Yes, this is critical of the church but I do not consider it a put down. I consider it a legitimate challenge to the church to study its belief system and practices within the process of morphing.

Then in my blog search I came to Blog 78. Can Creeds and Confessions Be Theistic?

In Blog 78, and in other blogs, especially Blog 81, I explore how the Presbyterian Church (USA) tries through its Constitution and parliamentary processes to instill spirituality into its membership. I quote from Blog 78:

"Laypersons cope with the volumes of material they are asked by our denomination (PCUSA) to absorb as confessions, creeds and theological constructs. I pose this question: Does my church grasp how much the addition of this confession will add to the contents of the box that I must leap beyond to find a viable spirituality that I can utilize in fulfilling my every-day existence?

Technically an atheist is one who does not believe in a theistic (directive) God. In that usage of the word I am an atheist. One who does not believe in any God would more accurately be an adeist – but this word does not exist. In a world that is coming to be more holistic than theistic, I would offer that the metaphysical force that renders purpose to total existence relates to all of life as the Atmosphere of Possibilities as opposed to a Library of Theism."

Yes, I am critical of excesses of verbiage but I do not consider that a put down. I consider it a legitimate challenge to the church to study its belief system and practices within the process of morphing.

83. A Leap to Spirituality.

Who determines the correct spirituality for me from among the many *spiritualities* within Christianity? . . . **I do**.

In the previous blog I asserted my change of direction via this statement;

"What does this mean? It means that it could make more sense for me to leap to rightness than to leap to a specific righteousness, i.e. a traditional faith. This sounds simplistic but instead it is a profound turning point in my search for validity in the quest to morph Christianity."

My leap is not merely to Presbyterianism (rule by elders). This is the institutional modality into which I was born and through which I demonstrate my leap to other humans. My leap is not to righteousness – there are too many forms of that. My leap is not to the God so distorted by human generated theism. My leap cannot be to some **incomprehensible** metaphysical force that I believe gives purpose to the all of existence. My leap is to a spirituality that I can utilize and fulfill within **my** every-day human existence - fully aware that on some days I will fail.

It has come to me over my years of connection with the church that we proclaim faith but practice manipulation. It has come to me more recently that the church praises diversity but demands unanimity in too many areas. At least some Presbyterians are all twisted out of shape over salvation, creeds, doctrines, tenets, Book of Order, ordination, sexual orientation, on and on. Some portions of the church haven't yet heard that there are movements afoot in human rights, e.g. civil, racial, gender.

So my change in direction is to believe that Christianity will morph when enough Christians leap to a viable spirituality.

84. What Is a Viable Spirituality?

"My leap is to a spirituality that I can utilize and fulfill within **my** every-day human existence."

My spirituality is of no value if it is expressed in verbiage that another cannot understand. But fortunately - persons who cannot understand my words can interpret my actions. "Could actions speak louder than words?" How do spiritual works compare with theistic faiths in everyday life?

It seems to me that a leap to viable spirituality is the preeminent possibility within the Atmosphere of Possibilities. Viable is one of my favorite words, but would the term viable spirituality be considered an oxymoron?

I remember growing up with Sunday clothes and everyday clothes. How would the term **everyday spirituality** serve as the preeminent possibility in our everyday existence?

85. God Is Moving in Our Time.

Recently I read an article on hunger and poverty that offered hope through the statement that "God is moving in our time to overcome hunger and poverty." With no intention of appearing bemused I shall express bemusement. I have no intent to tilt with riddles - but why would the metaphysical force that *perpetually* renders purpose to the all of existence make a specific, theistic "move in our time to overcome [*humanly created*] hunger and poverty?"

This is theism on an ultimately, non-productive scale. Supposedly God told humans in one eon, "Go forth and multiply." In later eons they have overdone it, and now, too many lack the universal compassion to help those who suffer due to the excessive, human propagation and the human-induced degradation of Earth's resources and climate.

Two essential human, participatory capabilities within the purpose for existence are **underutilized** by all of us humans:

1. Sufficient compassion if humans are to be responsible to all of humanity.
2. Sufficient spirituality if humans are to be response-able to the metaphysical purpose within all of existence. (God, or the Atmosphere of Possibilities, or _____ - reader's preference.)

Could the intentional utilization of these two possibilities as capabilities support the morphing of Christianity?

86. Compassion and Spirituality.

Could the intentional utilization of these two possibilities as capabilities support the morphing of Christianity?

When we base our answer on comprehensible climates of cultures and traditions (what has been) we must answer tentatively – "Maybe." When we base our answer on the incomprehensible Atmosphere of

157

Possibilities (what may become) we can be much more affirming. As I said earlier concerning the hard, green pear breaking the antique pane of etched glass – so much in life is relative.

Therefore my answer is, "Yes." I started establishing this affirmation way back in Blog 4. Here follows the summary statement of that blog as a quote:

"I believe that compassion (being responsible to/with fellow humans) was the first purpose for life discovered by the human and religious beliefs (being response-able to some metaphysical functionary) came eons later. Why, then, has the human forsaken the value and purposefulness of compassion that permitted humanity to evolve and survive, and has become obsessed with taking religious beliefs too seriously (e.g. religious chaos, religious wars)?"

Over the span of this two-year blog the reader will note that I have moved from the term religious beliefs, and a too serious abuse of them, to the term spirituality, and the inadequate use of it.

"Religious beliefs" and "spirituality" are entirely different entities. Over my years I have known many nominal Christians who wore several layers of religious beliefs applied over an inadequate primer coat of spirituality. These are the folks my friend describes as – "Way down deep they are really very shallow." On too many occasions I find myself fitting very easily into those shallow ranks.

We recognize that the evolution of physical life forms is a billion year process. How then can we select a 4,000 year blip of time and declare it to be the incubating instant of our religious beliefs? It has taken 2 million years for the human animal to become its still-changing, human, physical form. Compassion (as a possibility within the Atmosphere of Possibilities) has trudged every year of it with us. Is that patience, or what?

In contrast to comprehensible religious beliefs and incomprehensible spirituality being entirely different entities, compassion and spirituality are synergistic, like possibility genes side by side in the human genome. Of course I am speaking figuratively but I can grasp this metaphor more readily than I do the words of Summa Theologica ("the *perfect* description of God).

What -- if – we –

as kinetic molecules, could leap past the too religious to everyday spirituality in the Eternal Atmosphere of Possibilities?

Would – that – be – morphing?

Epilogue

As these blogs become a book, I transpose from a blogger to an author. Does this alter the authenticity of the material? I don't think so.

Any material is authentic and has value only if it speaks to the needs of the reader. As I have created these blogs I have referenced the needs and the responses of the blog's readers. Therefore this is not a "know it all" book nor is it of any value to those who already think they do (know it all). It is a "what I learned after I knew it all that really counts" book. By the way – I don't know for sure - did John Wooden or Earl Weaver originate that phrase?

Recently a person who had read a previous book of mine asked me when did I first start to sense the morphing of my belief system. I suggested that this question might be akin to Darwin asking a Galapagos Island finch when it first noticed its beak changing shape. Then I elaborated with a more reasonable explanation that morphing probably started when I became comfortable with the realization that I was uncomfortable with the orthodoxy my Christian tradition was directing me to accept.

Presently – inaccurate, Judeo-Christian, theistic traditions reinforced by intimidation comprise an axis quite capable of insinuating pseudo-guilt into those who would dare take the leap to morph their orthodox belief systems.

But -- this axis can be morphed when enough believers leap to Everyday Spirituality within the Atmosphere of Possibilities -- and Christianity can survive.

However – to paraphrase Elton Trueblood, "I am no doubt planting a tree in whose shade I will never rest."

So – I'll plant it anyway.

Justification -- I've tried to present ponderings as proofs rather than as personal rails or obsessions. (e.g. **78. Can Creeds and Confessions Be Theistic?**)

Affirmation -- It is my hope that I have presented my thoughts on matters deemed controversial as affirmation of my belief system and not as degradation of the belief systems of others.

Elinor and I shall continue to support the Presbyterian Congregation that we have been members of for 64 years and shall do so for our remaining years.

I shall just go blogging along and hope that somehow the Church comes to realize the difference between Everyday Spirituality and Biblical Faith and morphing steers Christianity to the conceptualization that the Eternal Atmosphere of Possibilities is more sustaining than a Library of Theism.

Glossary

ABCs in – "The box to be thought beyond:"
A. Factious Fundamentals and Doctrines.
B. Embellished Stories and Myths.
C. Outmoded Knowledge and Cultures.
ableness – a coined noun to express the state of being;e.g. response-able, response-ableness. See response-able.
agnostic – noun - a person who believes that nothing is known or can be known of the existence or nature of God or anything beyond material phenomena; a person who claims neither faith nor disbelief in God. There are many more agnostics than adeists and atheists.
adeism – noun – (coined word) belief that deism does not exist.
adeist – noun - (coined word) one who believes that the deistic God does not exist – to completely reject Traditional God one must be an adeist and an atheist. One can be an adeist and an atheist and still believe in the Metaphysical Force beyond deism and theism.
atheism – noun – the theory or belief that theism does not exist.
atheist – noun – one who believes that the theistic God does not exist.
Atmosphere of Possibilities – See Incomprehensible God.
belief system – the conceptualized system on which beliefs are based. For example a religious belief system is based on faith and dogma whereas a scientific belief system is based on observation and reason.
Charter for Compassion – A current statement to bring compassion to humanity as a confession of purpose.
Compassion Link – the place of compassion within human evolution.
Comprehensible God of the Bible Verse (the Climate of Cultures) - God as recorded in the writings of previous cultures.

(See Incomprehensible God of the Universe, the Atmosphere of Possibilities).

created-image humans - Biblical language states that the human is created in the image of God. If we can avoid the anthropomorphic conceptualization of God looking like a human (physical) and grasp the conceptualization of the human portraying some of God's love (spiritual) this term has valid use.

deism – noun – belief in the existence of a supreme being, specifically a creator who does not intervene in the universe. The term is used chiefly as an intellectual movement in the 17th and 18th centuries that accepted the existence of a creator on the basis of reason but rejected belief in a supernatural deity who interacts with humankind. Compare with theism.

deist – one who believes in deism.

dogma – a principle or set of principles laid down by an authority as incontrovertibly true.

encomium – a flattering statement that may or may not be true.

errant – deviating from the regular or proper course.

errancy – a coined noun to express a state of errant being.

evangelism – the human sharing of God's love within all of humanity.

faith - The traditional Nature of God is Love. Traditional faith is to be response-able to God.

Gnostic – noun - an adherent of Gnosticism.

Gnosticism – noun - a prominent heretical movement of the 2nd Century Christian Church, partly of pre Christian origin, Gnostic doctrine taught that the world was created and ruled by a lesser divinity, the demiurge, and that Christ was an emissary of the remote supreme divine being - esoteric knowledge (gnosis) of whom enabled the redemption of the human spirit.

God's business – theistic view, what God does is God's business.

Incomprehensible God of the Universe (the Atmosphere of Possibilities) – that beyond comprehension that lures humanity upslope to its spiritual potential. (See Comprehensible God of the Bible Verse, the Climate of Cultures)

inerrant – free from error; incapable of error.

informational nudge(s) – the metaphysical force in action giving purpose to existence.

innocent-errancy – a coined term to express the state of believing errant information innocently because it is the best explanation currently available. e.g. The world is flat (1491), the Biblical creation stories, the early concept that the Sun rotated around the Earth.

Innominate Society – four old geezers in conversation.

Kindom of God – a coined term to describe the relationship of all humans as being kin within God rather than subjects of God as a king. (Origin unknown)

kinetic molecule – size of each human in the Atmosphere of Possibilities.

Kingdom of God – a term used in ancient times to describe Heaven and Earth as the domain of God in human geopolitical terms. The term continues into the present age as a selective term for believers (those in the Kingdom) and non-believers (those outside the Kingdom).

Library of Theism – conceiving the metaphysical force that renders value and purpose to existence as human words rather than spiritual possibilities.

moral imagination – putting oneself in another's shoes – reciprocal altruism – the Golden Rule.

over-comprehend – to claim a faith beyond normal, healthy responseableness to God. e.g. to claim a relationship with God stronger than that of other created-image humans.

pinch of spirit in the human – a term borrowed from Arnold Toynbee's concept of the connectional relationship between Creator God and created humans.

Quinitarian – a modern, coined supposition that God functions as Creator, Sustainer, Redeemer, Mediator and Savior. (See Trinitarian)

relationships – the most powerful ships afloat.

religion – the belief in and worship of a superhuman controlling power, esp, a personal God or gods.- a particular system of faith or worship that connects the human to the superhuman.

response-able – the innate ability of every human to respond to God.

A more powerful concept than being responsible to God as a vaguely defined quality.

revelation-deprived – if there are times, places and persons to whom God makes disproportionate revelations, this would infer that God's Grace is disproportionate. It would infer that all other times, places and peoples are revelation-deprived. If God is Love, if God is Grace, how can there be revelation-deprivation?

spirituality – just as there is a metaphysical force that gives purpose to all of existence, pinches of that force give unique purpose to humans as they face their share of that existence every day. To be response-able within endless possibilities the human has the innate ability to leap to limitless everyday spirituality.

theism – noun – belief in the existence of a god or gods, esp. belief in one god as creator of the universe, intervening in it and sustaining a personal relation to "his" creatures. Compare with deism.

Trinitarian – an ancient doctrine that God exists in three forms: Father, Son and Holy Spirit.

uniquity – a noun coined from the adjective unique. e.g. That which is a uniquity, pl. uniquities.

worship – God is love within all of the universe and within all of humanity. **Omni worship** is humanity promising God to utilize that love in support of a fragile earth and mankind. **Theistic worship** is imploring God to break the natural laws of the universe to benefit the worshipper.

Suggested Readings

Abraham: A Journey to the Heart of Three Faiths
Perennial, Bruce Feiler

A Belief System from the General Store
Author House, Edgar K. DeJean

A Belief System from Beyond the Box
Author House, Edgar K. DeJean

Beyond Belief – the Secret Gospel of Thomas
Vintage Books, Elaine Pagels

Christianity, The First 3,000 Years.
Penguin Books, Diarmaid MacCulloch

Eternal Life: A New Vision
Harper One, John Shelby Spong

The Evolution of God
Little, Brown and Company, Robert Wright

Genes, Genesis, and God
Cambridge Univ. Press, Holmes Rolston, III

The God Delusion
Houghton-Miflin-Harcourt, Richard Dawkins

The Greatest Thing in the World
(Collins) Great Britain, Henry Drummond

If Grace Is True
Harper San Francisco, Phillip Gulley and James Mulholland

I Have a Dream
Grosset & Dunlap, Martin Luther King, Jr.

Man's Search for Himself
W. W. Norton and Co. Rollo May

Mark Twain's Religion
Mercer University Press, William E. Phipps

A New Earth
A Plume Book, Eckhart Tolle

Pale Blue Dot
Random House, Carl Sagan

The Phenomenon of Man
Harper and Row, N.Y. Teilhard de Chardin

Religious Inquiry
Philosophical Library, Holmes Rolston, III

Saving Creation, Nature and Faith in the Life of Holmes Rolston III
Trinity University Press, C. J. Preston

A Study of History
Oxford Univ. Press, N.Y. Arnold J. Toynbee

The Suicidal Church
Pluto Press Australia, Caroline Miley

Why Christianity Must Change or Die
Harper San Francisco, John Shelby Spong

Your God is Too Small
Simon Shuster, New York, J. B. Phillips

- - -

About the Author

How does an author tell a readership enough about himself/herself that readers acknowledge the writer as authentic?

How does a biography avoid an appearance of boasting?

How can a writer fulfill both of these requirements?

This writer believes himself to be an average church member adequately engaged in the mission of Christianity and of his particular denomination (Presbyterian USA) to write authentically to the church and to a general readership. He is a lifelong Presbyterian who has been an elder in his local church for over 60 years serving his share of duties vital to its continued existence. He has participated in the next higher judicatory (presbytery) as a frequent committee member, on multiple commissions, twice as moderator of presbytery plus as a delegate to multiple general assemblies.

A current, circulating admonition states: "Christianity must change or die." This writer's experiences lead him to observe that this is a credible concern. However his trust in the core values of Christianity as they can be practiced would soften that phrase to, "Christianity can morph and survive."

In the Robert Wright book, "The Evolution of God," the following quote summarizes the desperate need for morphing: "Any religion whose prerequisites for individual salvation don't conduce to the salvation of the whole world is a religion whose time has past."

Because this writer discerns hope that Christianity can morph and survive to "conduce to the salvation of the whole world" does not mean that he is boasting that it will be easy or that he knows how to effect it. It means that he sees it as a preeminent possibility to be fulfilled within Atmosphere of Possibilities.

Author's e-mail addresses:

<edejean@blueriver.net>   <edgardejean@gmail.com>